The Cop Critics

BY DANIEL BURKE

DORRANCE PUBLISHING CO
EST. 1920
PITTSBURGH, PENNSYLVANIA 15238

Dorrance Publishing Co
585 Alpha Drive
Suite 103
Pittsburgh, PA 15238
Visit our website at www.dorrancebookstore.com

ISBN: 979-8-88812-201-3
eISBN: 979-8-88812-701-8

The Cop Critics

TABLE OF CONTENTS

FOOD FOR THOUGHT

"It is not the critic who counts; not the man who points out how the strong man stumbles, or where the doer of deeds could have done them better. The credit belongs to the man who is actually in the arena, whose face is marred by dust and sweat and blood; who strives valiantly; who errs, who comes short again and again, because there is no effort without error and shortcoming; but who does actually strive to do the deeds; who knows great enthusiasms, the great devotions; who spends himself in a worthy cause; who at the best knows in the end the triumph of high achievement, and who at the worst, if he fails, at least fails while daring greatly, so that his place shall never be with those cold and timid souls who neither know victory nor defeat." Theodore Roosevelt

"Thou hypocrite, first cast out the beam out of thine own eye; and then shalt thou see clearly to cast out the mote out of thy brother's eye." Jesus Christ, Matthew 7:5, KJV

A FEW DEFINITIONS

Cop: Origin disputed. Possibly an acronym for Constable On Patrol. Possibly a reference to early police badges being made of copper. Possibly from an old Anglo-Saxon verb, "cop," meaning grab or capture. Unless context dictates otherwise in this work, the word, "cop," refers to male or female municipal, county, or state law enforcement officers and is interchangeable with the word, "officer." For the sake of brevity, when referring to cop or officer, the personal pronouns he, his, or him can refer to male or female law enforcement officers.

As used in this work, the word "Gender" refers to biological and genetic markers that distinguish males from females. The author does not recognize modern social/cultural constructs of self-determined gender identity or gender fluidity. The word "Race" originally referred to Human Race, i.e. homo sapiens: bipedal primates with large, complex brains, and the development of advanced tools, culture, and language. Unfortunately, modern social and cultural forces have corrupted the term to refer to skin color. So, unless context dictates otherwise, that is how it is used it in this work.

WHY THIS BOOK?

Cops have endured unfair criticism for decades. That criticism has reached an ugly and irrational fever pitch. Our critics don't paint us with a broad brush. They use high volume industrial sprayers with no regard for the collateral damage they do in the process. So I thought it was time to return the favor.

I began portions of this work before I retired from law enforcement. I poured enough of my blood, sweat, and tears into the profession to still consider myself a remote part of it. And, since some of my friends and associates are still employed in the profession and have given me their permission to speak on their behalf, I sometimes use first person pronouns when referring to cops.

It is not my proposition that cops are perfect. We know we're not. We're human. And, just like our critics, we sometimes make honest human mistakes. On rare occasions years of job stress breaks a cop's moral compass and he does some dreadful deed that he wouldn't have dreamed of doing when he began his career. Sometimes a bad apple slips through the narrow cracks in the hiring process. But those are exceptions that do not represent the bulk of our members. I had numerous professional and personal disagreements with coworkers, supervisors, and administrators during my career. Most off those disagreements were "in-house debates" concerning department operations, policies, or procedures. Those disagreements and debates did not impact the services received by the public. What critics are so quick to consider intentional acts of malice by "bad cops" are more often honest miscalculations made during explosive circumstances that were set in motion by a criminal suspect. Such a miscalculation by a cop can result in a tidal wave of calamities that last a lifetime. A comparable miscalculation by someone in almost any other profession would cause only a momentary ripple of inconvenience.

Like human beings in every other walk of life, cops have their own individual personalities, strengths, weaknesses, imperfections, and quirks. Nevertheless, the overwhelming majority of them do the job honorably, even if imperfectly. In spite of that, our critics promote the narrative that our profession is riddled with devilish corruption and brutality. That narrative is pure unadulterated bullshit. The critics who promote that narrative are either pathological liars or virtual morons. There is no third option. Those in the first category use that narrative to promote their toxic social and political agendas, and to emotionally manipulate people in the second category into believing the narrative. When our critics do occasionally speak well of us, it is only insincere virtue signaling to mask their true contempt.

Who am I to criticize the critics? During my twenty-five years in law enforcement, I attended dozens of seminars, workshops, and training classes. I worked as a patrol officer and as a criminal investigator. I worked for multiple municipal, county, and state law enforcement agencies. I was a field training officer and an adjunct instructor at a regional public service academy for more than a decade. I have been a licensed private investigator and investigation agency owner for thirty years. On top of that, I have personal and professional experiences interacting with and observing people in each of the categories of critics that I identify.

I can't count the number of occasions I tried to have rational discussions with the critics about their mistaken beliefs. Those efforts were fruitless and reminded me of a 1778 comment that Thomas Paine published about Sir William Howe, Commander of British land forces in the Colonies during the American War of Independence:

"To argue with a man who has renounced the use and authority of reason, and whose philosophy consists in holding humanity in contempt, is like administering medicine to the dead, or endeavoring to convert an atheist by scripture."

I spent years trying to figure out what was behind that intransigent contempt. I finally realized that their contempt is not due to anything we do or fail to do. It is a contempt born of jealousy and guilt. Jealousy, because they know that the measurable benefit they provide to society pales in comparison to ours. Guilt, because they know they are unworthy of the idolatrous accolades they receive for the negligible benefit they actually do provide. They sooth their craven consciences by the defense mechanisms of deflection and projection; they deflect attention away from their own loathsome character traits by projecting those traits onto us. They are angry and mean-spirited Lilliputians trying to hatchet flawed but benevolent Gulliver's down to their own size.

My purpose in this book is not so much to sling some well-deserved mud back at our critics as it is to educate and warn the non-critics and the undecided about their own vulnerability to the Machiavellian manipulation that the critics use to try to win converts to their cop hating cult.

With a few exceptions, I purposely avoid identifying our critics by name in this work for two reasons. One is I want you to focus more on the general comments and philosophies of the critics within the context of their behaviors and lifestyles rather than focus on their personal identities. The other is that I don't want to get into protracted arguments with publishing house attorneys about my comments being libelous. Not naming individuals precludes that argument from happening.

Finally, since cops are at the mercy of politicians, many of whom spend every waking moment trying to exploit the critics for political gain, that gives me license to call some of the politicians out as the hypocrites that they truly are.

WHO ARE THE COPS CRITICS?

If I could use only one word to describe the cop critics, the word would be "imbeciles." Most retired veteran cops agree with me. So do most currently employed veteran cops. The difference is that those still employed can't say so publicly because they fear being fired if they do. That fear is well-founded. Dozens of officers in the past decade have been fired for publicly expressing their opinions either verbally, or in writing, or on the internet. It did not matter that their opinions were expressed off-duty, or that the opinions did not threaten anyone, did not advocate doing unlawful violence to anyone, and did not advocate depriving anyone of any constitutional right. The opinions were just sarcastic, sardonic, or satirical rants that were brought on by having to deal with the massive failures of the criminal justice system and the stunning stupidity of the people who go through that system with alarming regularity. Nevertheless, some sanctimonious critic was offended by the rant and complained about it to some bureaucrat in a position of authority over the officer. The critic who complained was likely an incarnation of the stupidity described in the officer's rant. The bureaucrat who entertained the complaint was likely an incompetent nitwit who got his or her job by nepotism, personal friendship, or political fellatio. The bureaucrat, being as stupid as the critic, declared the officer's comments to be "unacceptable" and fired the officer to appease the critic.

This tyrannical power by government bureaucrats has effectively blackmailed cops into surrendering their constitutional right to free speech as a condition for employment. Since cops are on the front lines in the war on crime and are intimately acquainted with the causes and results of that crime, a sensible person would think that the opinions of cops should be given serious consideration by politicians and other government policy makers. But cops are not diplomats. They're soldiers who tend to express their opinions in battlefield jargon that critics find offensive. The critics then use their considerable financial, political, or social influence to prevent the officers' opinions from getting a fair hearing. Then they try to destroy the careers of officers who dare to express opinions that do not conform to the critics' "woke" social and political ideologies. They take an officer's comments out of context and twist it to imply that the officer's opinions are a reflection of some personal prejudice or animosity. The fact that an officer's comments were objectively accurate, and there was no evidence that the officers' professional performance was ever influenced by any personal prejudice or animosity, is irrelevant to critics. Critics believe that even having personal prejudices or animosities irreparably taints every action an officer takes and disqualifies him from service. The International Association of Chiefs of Police does not appear to agree with the critics. The proof of that is contained in the IACP Law Enforcement Code of Ethics. Paragraph three of that code, at least the one that was in effect throughout most of my career, says:

"I will never act officiously or permit personal feelings, prejudices, animosities or friendships to influence my decisions."

That paragraph implicitly presupposes that cops, like everyone else, have personal prejudices and animosities. But it also presupposes that cops have the intellectual and moral capacity to perform their duties without being influenced by those prejudices and animosities. Officers who do not have that capacity usually don't last long. They quit or get fired. In truth, officer actions that critics think are motivated by personal prejudice or animosity are nearly always objective professional judgment calls that are based upon state statute, case law, hundreds of hours of training, personal observations, and years of real world experience.

A CLOSER LOOK

To be more specific about our critics, they are arrogant elitists who are hellbent on promoting their delusional social and political agendas by subjugating or silencing anyone who disagrees with them. How do these critics hunt their prey? Like a pack of wild hyenas. How do they make a living? Most of them are movie and television celebrities, broadcast and print news journalists, professional sports celebrities, college and university professors, and self-appointed social justice warriors (SJWs). The remaining critics fall into the category of mentally challenged or morally bankrupt souls who are either unable or unwilling to conform to simple laws that only require them to abstain from doing things that are harmful or potentially harmful to other people. I am not saying that everyone in any of those categories is a cop critic. A small percentage of those people actually appreciate what we do and we're grateful for their support. It would be nice if they were a little more outspoken with that support, but I understand why they aren't. They would be professionally black-listed and socially ostracized if they were. But the fact remains that our most vocal and vitriolic critics fall into at least one of those categories.

Aside from their arrogance and hypocrisy, our critics have something else in common. They suffer from the "Dunning-Kruger Effect." The Dunning-Kruger Effect is a phrase coined by psychologists David Dunning and Justin Kruger based upon their 1999 study titled "Unskilled and Unaware of It: How Difficulties in Recognizing One's Own Incompetence Lead to Inflated Self-

Assessments." That study describes how people with limited knowledge or competence in a given intellectual or social domain greatly overestimate their own knowledge or competence in that domain relative to objective criteria.

Our critics consider themselves experts in their respective professions, and they resent having their professional judgment or performance criticized by anyone who lacks their expertise. Yet, in spite of having no training or experience in law enforcement, never having made an arrest, or been in a gun fight, or been in a high speed pursuit, or been in a fight for their life with a violent criminal, or inhaled the stench of decaying human flesh at a week old crime scene, or been pelted with blow flies while loading a decaying carcass into a body bag, or been spattered with blood while trying to save the life of someone who moments earlier tried to kill them and was a virtual cornucopia of potentially deadly pathogens, our critics use their bully pulpits to publicly criticize our professional performance in terms that ooze with personal contempt. In the current cancel culture, created and jealously guarded by the critics, we have few platforms from which we can refute their criticisms. And they certainly aren't going to give us one, or acknowledge even the possibility that they are mistaken. A book is about the only platform we have left. As I go through this work, I will occasionally relate some personal anecdotes that I think are useful to illustrate various points.

WHAT DO THE CRITICS LOOK LIKE?

It depends upon who you ask. The critics see themselves as intellectually and spiritually illuminated beings who are making the world a better place. We see them as narcissistic morons who are turning the world into a stinking shithole. The stench from that hole never rises to the rarefied atmosphere that the critics live and work in. They only view it in two dimensions from a safe distance. Our critics' collective contribution to societal tranquility can only be measured in British Thermal Units, Cubic Feet Per Minute, or Pounds Per Square Inch. They snipe at us from the safety of movies and television dramas, talk shows, tabloids, awards ceremonies, sporting events, college classrooms, protest rallies, internet blogs, etc. But they don't have the guts to take our deadly risks, make our mind-bending split-second decisions, endure our stress-induced diseases, accept our shortened life expectancy, or carry the burden of our professional code of ethics. A burden, by the way, that would snap their collective moral and ethical backbone like a dry twig in a cattle stampede. Let's look at these critics in their natural element.

HOORAY FOR HOLLYWOOD

Celebrities in various positions within the "entertainment" branch of the movie and television industry detest us. They publicly support defunding the police. They proudly attach their highly recognizable names to letters and petitions that promote emotionally inflammatory lies about us. Here is an example of a few of those lies from one such letter:

"Despite continued profiling, harassment, terror and killing of Black communities, local and federal decision-makers continue to invest in the police, which leaves Black people vulnerable and our communities no safer."

The combined estimated net worth of just three of the celebrities who signed that letter is three hundred and sixty-five million dollars. None of those celebrities live or work in the communities that they falsely claim to care so much about. When the people who do live in those communities call 911 for help, they expect us to instantly appear like the genie from Aladdin's lamp to magically solve whatever real or imagined problem prompted them to call.

Our critics support organizations and initiatives that advocate restricting or eliminating private ownership of firearms, abolishing the death penalty, replacing prisons with mental health clinics and social service programs, and allowing unfettered entry into the US by anyone who wants to come in. If you're an average law abiding citizen who cannot afford to live in a celebrity mansion in a gated community with twenty-four hour armed security, or travel around in private jets and chauffeured limousines, do you think those organizations and initiatives make you and your loved ones safer? Some of those celebrities provide moral and financial support to violent and well known anarchist and Marxist organizations. What those celebrities lack in common sense they more than make up for in their craving for attention; a craving that responsible adults outgrew before graduating from high school. But instead of outgrowing that craving, the celebrities nurtured it until they became full-grown adults with full-blown anti-social, borderline, histrionic, or narcissistic personality disorders. You think not? Then think about how often you hear of wealthy movie and television celebrities, both male and female, white and black, young and old, being charged with DUI, battery, drug possession, domestic violence, disorderly conduct, rape, assault, fleeing from police, soliciting prostitutes, resisting arrest, or some other cluster B behavior. Think about how often you hear of them checking themselves into drug or alcohol rehab, or into psychiatric clinics. Think about how often you hear of them being involved in marital infidelity, pedophilia, sexual deviance, drug overdose, or suicide. Think about how often you hear of them living for decades as millionaires, only to finish their lives in bankruptcy because they squandered their wealth on unbridled hedonism. Think of how often you hear of their neglected or misguided children suffering from drug or alcohol addiction, manic depression, gender dysphoria, drug overdose or suicide. The psychological instabilities of these celebrities is legendary, and the damage they do to nearly everyone they touch is immeasurable. But they consider themselves intellectually and morally qualified to criticize cops.

Where did their psychological instabilities come from? They had those instabilities long before they were celebrities. In fact, it was those instabilities that drove them to seek celebrity status in the first place. Read some of their bios. When they were children they sang, danced, belched, cartwheeled, yelled, or did almost anything else for attention. In school they were cheerleaders, thespians, class clowns, class trouble makers, bullies, vandals, etc. If they went to college, they majored in performing arts or journalism, and they minored in substance abuse, promiscuity, partying, protesting, or anything else that would gratify their craving for attention. Some of them actually admit that they wanted to be actors, actresses, writers, directors, rock stars, or have some other connection with the entertainment industry so badly that they nearly starved to death to pursue that dream. That insatiable craving for attention might be momentarily amusing in a six year-old, but it is a major red flag for serious psychological problems in adults. And it is that craving for attention that prevents them from keeping their mouths shut about subjects that they are totally unqualified to speak about, such as law enforcement.

Celebrity critics loudly condemn us as racists when a violent criminal, who only coincidentally happens to be black, instigates a confrontation that requires us to use a level of force that results in the criminal being injured or killed. If the criminal happens to be white, and many of them are, the celebrities have little to say about it because that would take attention away from their false narrative of systemic racism. Critics don't care that the amount of force we use is based on the level of resistance or aggression displayed by the person we're arresting; not on the color of that person's skin. Cops use only the level of force needed to get the job done while trying to avoid injury to themselves. Critics ignore the details that led to the confrontation. They disregard the violent history of the criminal in question. They don't know the legal definition of excessive force. And they don't know the amount of real-world force that is actually required to subdue someone who is violently resisting.

The celebrity critics proudly put their hypocrisy on public display by feigning horror over news reports of officers injuring or killing suspects who are involved in violent acts. But they write, produce, direct, or star in movies and television shows that are saturated with violence that is gratuitous enough to make a serial killer vomit. Watch a few of their cop movies and television shows from the past couple of decades. Look at the advertising trailers and posters for those movies and television shows. Consider how many of those movies, television shows, trailers and posters depict celebrity cop characters recklessly brandishing or firing guns. Then ask yourself, "What kind of depraved mind writes, produces, directs, or stars in this nauseatingly violent trash?"

Fictional movie and television cops egregiously violate the rights of fictional suspects. They indiscriminately spray make-believe bullets in carefully choreographed gunfights with bad guys. Their stand-in stunt-drivers and stuntmen perform well planned and rehearsed car chases and physical fights that, after being meticulously edited and digitally manipulated, defy the laws of physics and exceed the capacities of human anatomy. They call this cinematic excrement "art." Some of you call it "entertainment." A foolish few of you worship these celebrities as gods. If we did in reality a small fraction of the stuff done by them in their cop movies and television shows, we would be fired and our law enforcement certifications would be revoked. We would end up either greeting people at the entrance of some giant discount department store, or cutting grass on the side of a rural highway under the supervision of a man carrying a rifle and wearing a Stetson and mirrored sunglasses. ("Shakin' the bush, boss. Shakin' the bush.")

So, before you good citizens let the celebrities use their admittedly persuasive charms to hypnotize you into believing the lies they spread about us, spend a few minutes seriously thinking about these differences between the celebrities who propagandize you, and the real cops who protect you.

Their faces are covered with Max Factor. Ours are covered with stress furrows. Their hair is colored by L'Oréal. Ours is prematurely gray or gone from the systemic shock of chronic adrenaline overload. Their scripts are crafted by professional writers in air conditioned offices. We spontaneously improvise our own in a furnace of life-threatening adversity. They wear haute couture from famous designers. We wear polyester and Kevlar from the low bidder. They dine on haute cuisine in fancy restaurants. We inhale fast-food from drive-thru windows. They live in multi-million dollar mansions in gated communities. We're your next-door neighbors. Their kids go to private schools. Our kids sit beside yours in public schools. Their gunfights are fake. Ours are real. They get rehearsals, stunt doubles and multiple takes to get it right. We get no rehearsals, no stand-ins, and no second chances. If they make a mistake, a director says "Cut!" If we make a mistake, the only cut we're likely to get is from a trauma surgeon or a medical examiner. Their awards are golden statues presented to them while their colleagues applaud and an orchestra plays the theme from their latest movie or television show. Ours is a folded flag presented to our next of kin while our colleagues weep and a bugler plays "Taps." They make millions in weeks to create mind-numbing garbage. We make thirty to sixty thousand a year to be falsely accused, frivolously sued, physically assaulted, or shot by people that celebrities think are victims of police brutality.

Those celebrities aren't your friends. They couldn't care less about your personal well-being. The criminals they defend as victims of police brutality are the same revolving-door recidivists who burglarize your homes, steal your cars, rob your businesses, murder your loved ones, vandalize your property, sell drugs to your kids, or have outstanding warrants for their arrest. And, contrary to what the celebrities would like you to believe, those criminals do not commit those crimes because they were marginalized or disenfranchised by an uncaring society. They do it for profit, or for the sheer pleasure they derive from terrorizing other human beings.

IF IT BLEEDS, IT LEADS!

The modern mainstream news media is a seamless extension of the movie and television entertainment industry. It has become nearly impossible to tell where one ends and the other begins. Modern so-called "news journalists" are the ideologically incestuous cousins of movie and television celebrities. If they were not competing for ratings or circulation numbers in news broadcasts and publications, they would be equally at home selling fad diets and unnecessary kitchen gadgetry to obese insomniacs on late night infomercials. A hundred and fifty years ago these modern-day carpetbaggers would have been selling snake oil from the back of a mule-drawn peddler's wagon. Be they print, cable, or broadcast, their unwritten motto is the same: "If it bleeds, it leads!"

If someone accuses us of brutality or some other professional impropriety, journalists will put us on trial in the court of public opinion while they withhold exculpatory evidence that would exonerate us in a real court. Their court has more in common with a tribunal by a despotic third world dictatorship. Journalists have no statutory oversight. We can't appeal or get a new trial when we're unjustly convicted because of their skewed presentation. The most we might get out of them is a two-line correction on a back page that no one reads, or a five-second correction at the end of a news broadcast when viewers have gone to the privy. The judges who oversee those trials are the journalists' collusive news directors and editors who play from the same page of politically radical music.

If you pay attention, you might notice that when an officer kills a suspect who was violently resisting arrest, mainstream news journalists will find a way to insert a human interest element into the story to make you believe that the suspect's behavior was somehow related to being a victim of childhood neglect, mental illness, or drug addiction. You see? It isn't about giving you only the relevant facts that would lead you to the obvious conclusion that the suspect's unlawful violent conduct was the proximate cause of his death. It's about emotionally manipulating you into having sympathy for the suspect and doubts about the motives of the officer who dispatched him. Journalists couldn't care less about the personal distress an officer suffers for having to snuff out the life of another human being, regardless of how wretched that life was, or how well justified the officer was in taking it. The officer eats that meal alone at a table for one.

Eliciting emotional responses, such as sympathy or anger, are the primary tools journalists use to manipulate viewers or readers into turning off the uniquely human capacity for objective critical thought. Emotions are the path of least resistance in manipulating people. And having an emotional response requires no effort; only the absence of resistance to it. The more emotionally fired-up journalists can cause people to become, the less likely those people are to engage in objective critical thought. Emotionally fired-up people do stupid things that the journalists can report on. Then other people watch or read those reports and get emotionally fired-up. In turn, they go out and do stupid things. So you now have a news industry that creates an atmosphere that produces an endless stream of news stories that will keep ratings and circulation up and keep the journalists gainfully employed.

One of the first things you do when you get up in the morning is turn on a television news broadcast to find out what happened in the world while you slept. The broadcast begins. The studio lighting and set colors are hallucinogenic and hypnotic. The music intros are loud and rhythmic. The anchors and field reporters are nauseatingly bubbly women who look like post-wall hookers or Hustler centerfolds. The few male anchors and reporters that are still in the business look like androgynous metrosexuals or Calvin Klein underwear models. And, in spite of having degrees in journalism, many of these anchors and field reporters struggle to put together an intelligible sentence without mispronouncing words or using pop culture jargon. They deliver the news with an excessive and annoying dose of their own infectious personal angst or enthusiasm to engage the viewers emotionally rather than intellectually. Just try to sit through a television news broadcast without the anchors and reporters mucking or yucking it up with their own childish banter, heavy sighs, furrowed brows, emotional inflections, or editorial musings. The evening news programs are a repeat of the morning programs with different anchors. But the manipulation tactics are the same. Emotional manipulation is the standard practice for modern journalists. But this tactic has been an industry standard for decades. Here are several examples that illustrate the point.

In the early 1990s a major television network produced a news segment that addressed automotive critics' charges that a major US auto manufacturer's trucks had a design flaw that would result in fire if the trucks were struck in a side-impact collision. The broadcast video of the program's crash test showed the truck erupting into spectacular flames when a car struck the side of it. The imagery was startling. Wow! Who would want to buy one of those trucks! But the manufacturer conducted its own investigation and discovered that network employees at the test site had rigged the truck's fuel tank with remotely controlled incendiary devices to initiate the explosion. A frame by frame examination of the video tape footage showed smoke from those devices coming from underneath the truck a fraction of a second before impact. The manufacturer also discovered that the gas tank was overfilled, the gas tank neck had the wrong cap on it, and the impact did not make a hole in the tank as alleged in the broadcast. The manufacturer sued the network. The network backed down by having two of its good looking popular journalists deliver the following statement:

"[Network's] contractor did put incendiary devices under the trucks to ensure that there would be a fire if gasoline were released from the trucks gas tank. We said the crash "forced gasoline to spew from the fuel cap." [the manufacturer] says since the gas cap was the wrong cap for the [manufacturer's] filler tube and because the gas tank was overfilled, the cap came off when the impact occurred. We agree with [the manufacturer] that we should have told our viewers about these devices. The [program] reporter however said, "at impact a small hole was punctured in the tank." [manufacturer] has now x-rayed that tank and found no hole. We acknowledge the placing of the incendiary devices under the truck was a bad idea from start to finish. That's our new policy."

That statement was nothing but ambiguous obfuscation, no doubt crafted by some network lawyer who got his moral compass from a box of Crackerjacks. As for the journalists involved in the crash test, we're not talking about overzealous thirteen year-old geeks fudging on a middle school science fair project. We're talking about educated adult employees of the news division of one of the world's largest broadcast corporations. Do you honestly believe that those employees did not understand that planting the incendiary devices was deceptive? Do you honestly think the network would have publicly apologized for the deception if it had not been discovered by the manufacturer?

In another case, a major television network news division broadcast a carefully edited excerpt from the recording of the 911 call that George Zimmerman made to the Sanford Police Department in the now famous 2012 George Zimmerman / Trayvon Martin incident in which Zimmerman shot and killed Martin. Here is the edited excerpt that the network broadcast multiple times:

> **Zimmerman to 911 operator:** "This guy looks like he's up to no good. He looks black."

Here is the unedited excerpt from that recording.

> **Zimmerman to 911 operator:** "This guy looks like he's up to no good. Or he's on drugs or something. It's raining and he's just walking around, looking about."
>
> **911 operator:** "OK, and this guy — is he black, white or Hispanic?"
>
> **Zimmerman:** "He looks black."

Do you honestly believe that the broadcast version was not intentionally edited to incite anger by trying to make it appear that Zimmerman's 911 call and the subsequent shooting were racially motivated rather than circumstantially motivated as clearly suggested in the unedited version? As in the previous case, when figuratively caught with its hand in the cookie jar, the network launched an investigation. Several journalists lost their jobs over the incident, and the network issued this so called "apology":

"During our investigation it became evident that there was an error made in the production process that we deeply regret. We will be taking the necessary steps to prevent this from happening in the future and apologize to our viewers."

More ambiguity and obfuscation! The only thing the network deeply regretted was being caught with its proverbial fly unzipped. It probably didn't occur to them that someone might actually compare the full 911 recording to their edited version. Most professional news journalists have degrees or college level training in journalism. They are highly skilled in the use of words, what those words mean in a given context, and how those words will be understood by the listener or the reader. Do you honestly believe that the journalists who edited the 911 recording did not know precisely what they were doing? Do you honestly believe that they were not trying to emotionally manipulate viewers by promoting their own unsupportable toxic presuppositions and social agenda? Regardless of any news outlet's so called "apologies," that which has been seen or heard cannot be unseen or unheard. First impressions are lasting impressions. There is no way to accurately measure how many people formed an irreversibly negative opinion of the truck manufacturer as a result of the first story. Likewise, there is no way to measure the irreversible unjustified personal hatred that the deceptively edited 911 recording engendered towards Zimmerman. Unfortunately for the public, malicious journalists who get fired from one news outlet are often hired by other news outlets elsewhere because the bosses who fire them do so reluctantly, and only to avoid potential embarrassment if they do not. But those bosses also give them good recommendations for other journalistic employment. Why? Because the bosses have the same unsupportable toxic presuppositions and social agendas that the fired journalists have. How many other acts of journalistic malice and malfeasance go undiscovered or unchallenged because the injured party was either not smart enough to realize that he had been publicly libeled by journalists, or because he didn't have the financial clout to battle the legions of lawyers employed by massive broadcasting corporations and publishers? The two cases I mentioned are just the tip of the iceberg.

Emotional manipulation to incite anger or to influence public opinion is systemic in the mainstream news industry. The news media's main objective is not simply to make the public aware of newsworthy events. It is to psychologically manipulate viewers into adopting the political and social views of the journalists. A secondary goal is to profit by starting wars between peoples of different colors, different cultures, or different socioeconomic classes. The journalists then fan the flames in those wars by providing lopsided coverage. Were it not for the news media intentionally starting those wars or fanning the flames, most of the combatants would eventually get tired, call a truce, go home, and get on with their lives. Eventually they would come to realize that the people who they were previously at war with were people who, like themselves, were just trying to pay their bills and take care of their families. Eventually those people would realize that their differences were fewer than they had been manipulated into believing and were not worth fighting about. They might even start getting along with each other. They might even become friends. Good Heavens! What would the news media have to report on then?

Whatever your color, your ethnicity, your age, or your socioeconomic class, you must stay constantly vigilant to keep yourself from being emotionally manipulated by the news media. Sometimes that manipulation can be seen as much by what they don't tell you as what they do tell you. Here are two examples that work together to illustrate that point.

In November of 1988, a convicted felon was released from prison after serving only eight years of a fifteen year sentence for attempted murder. Ten days after his release he murdered two law enforcement officers within seconds of each other by shooting them to death with their own guns during a single violent encounter in which he was able to disarm them. Two months later and fifteen miles away, in January of 1989, a law enforcement officer stepped into the street to intercept a motorcyclist who was fleeing from another officer. When the motorcyclist saw the officer standing in the street, he swerved toward the officer. The officer fired his duty weapon. The driver died instantly from the gunshot. The motorcycle went down and his passenger died from injuries in the crash. In January of 1990, the officer who shot the motorcyclist went on trial for manslaughter. A local television network affiliate preempted its daytime programming to broadcast gavel to gavel coverage of the officer's trial. In September of 1990, in the same courthouse, the man who murdered the two officers went on trial for murder. The only coverage the same network affiliate gave to that trial were brief updates of daily trial activity near the end of its evening news broadcasts. What was the difference in these two cases? The convicted felon was a black male, and the two officers he killed were white males. The fleeing motorcyclist was a black male, and the officer who shot him was a white Hispanic male. I called the affiliate and spoke with a man who identified himself as their news director. I told him that I thought their coverage of the two trials was biased and unbalanced. I told him that I thought the trial of a convicted felon who murdered two police officers ten days after being released seven years early from prison was just as important for the public to see as was the trial of a police officer who shot and killed a fleeing motorcyclist who was threatening to run him down. In spite of that conversation occurring more than thirty years ago, I remember the news director's terse reply as though the conversation happened this morning. You would do well to remember his reply each and every time you watch or read a news story. He said, "We decide what's important for the public to see!" That arrogance is pervasive within the broadcast and print news industry. That might not be a problem if journalists had a working moral compass and unbiased intentions. But they don't. Do an internet search for "news journalists who lie." Some of those journalists were well known network anchors with long careers. Others were lesser known local short timers trying to make a name for themselves. Imagine all of the undiscovered lies spread by those journalists before they were caught. Imagine all of the manipulative lying journalists whose dirty little lies have yet to be discovered. Either way, modern news journalists are just as morally and ethically qualified to decide what's important for you to see as Josef Mengele and Margaret Sanger would have been to run a pediatric hospital.

Another means by which the entertainment and news industry manipulates the public is via advertising. While that manipulation might not have a direct relationship to law enforcement, it does have an indirect relationship by short-circuiting the viewers' moral faculties and natural ability to distinguish between fact and fiction, reality and fantasy.

When people aren't working, they are probably spending way too much time watching television programs or internet videos. Those programs and videos are paid for by advertisements that are shown every few minutes. If you were to watch television commercials from the late fifties through the early eighties (since there was no internet), you would notice that the visual perspectives in those commercials was consistent with what your eyes would see in daily life. People dining, having conversations, traveling on public transportation, conducting business in stores, etc. Those commercials were filmed in real time from one or two angles and at distances that would reflect what you would see as an onlooker if you were actually there. Background music was either absent or subtle and played on acoustic instruments. My personal favorite is the 1969 Alka Seltzer "Spicy Meatball" commercial with Jack Somack. Another classic is the 1981 "FedEx" commercial with John Moschitta. Compare those commercials with what you see today. Extreme closeups and multiple camera angles that you would never experience in real life. Image changes that occur rapidly within fractions of seconds. Background music from electric and digital instruments that is loud and distorted. I just watched two commercials. One was for a local furniture store. The other was for a chain of casinos. Each commercial was fifteen seconds. In the furniture commercial the images changed nine times. In the casino commercial the image changed twenty times. In both commercials the narrator was practically yelling to overcome the background music. What's happening in these programs and commercials? The information is being fed through your eyes and ears so rapidly and explosively that your brain doesn't have the capacity to process or analyze it objectively. It gets stored in its raw form until some future stimulus causes you dredge it up and mentally play it again. And when you do, it will be in the same raw and unrealistic format that it was stored in, and you probably won't even realize it. Here's another devious example of how these manipulation techniques work. Closely watch the next prescription medicine commercial you see on television. When it gets to the part where the narrator starts listing all of the possible negative side effects, pay close attention to his or her voice, the background music, and the images. His or her voice and delivery will be soft and pleasant. The background music will be in a major key and upbeat time signature that evokes happiness and confidence. The video images will be in slow motion showing people laughing or smiling in some romantic or fun recreational activity. All three of those elements are contrary to the narrator's message that the medicine being advertised could kill you. But people will naturally associate the pleasant voice, upbeat music and happy images with a favorable outcome rather than death. In nearly every movie, television show, news program, or product commercial you see, the images, the music and the messages will have a troubling dissonance when compared to what you experience in the real world. People whose brains have been so conditioned to anticipate unrealistic outcomes will naturally rebel against the objective realities of dealing law enforcement officer encounters or actions.

Lest you think these are just my half-baked opinions, I would refer you to a well-researched book on the subject. "The Hidden Persuaders," by Vance Packard, was originally published in 1957. But in light of the major advances in audio and video technology since then, it is even more relevant today than it was when it was published. The New Yorker magazine described it as "A brisk, authoritative and frightening report on how manufacturers, fundraisers and politicians are attempting to turn the American mind into a kind of catatonic dough that will buy, give or vote at their command." No matter how smart you think you are, you are not immune from these subliminal manipulation tactics.

Here are just two personal anecdotes from my many interactions with news journalists. Circa 2007, a city council meeting was held at a recreation center because the city council chamber was not big enough to accommodate the number of people expected to attend. Because the recreation center had an occupancy limit, a fire department official was posted inside to monitor the number of occupants. I was posted at the front door to restrict entrance. When people inside wanted to leave, they were guided to a rear exit. The fire official would then call me on the radio and tell me how many people I could allow to come inside. As I stood at my post, I recognized a television reporter from local network affiliate pushing his way through the crowd of waiting citizens. He was followed by his cameraman. When he got to the entrance, he reached for the door as though I was not there. I stepped in front of him and told him that he would have to wait to go inside. He turned red and began yelling at me that he was a member of the press and that he had a first amendment right to go in, and that I had no right to stop him. I explained the occupancy restrictions, but he didn't care. He again demanded entry. I again denied him. He was furious. He threatened to sue me and the department for violating his first amendment right as a member of the press. His poor cameraman looked humiliated. I told the reporter to go ahead and sue me, but he was not going in until the fire official authorized it. Why would a news reporter be so belligerent towards a police officer who was only performing a basic public safety function? Because members of the media view themselves as a morally and intellectually elevated class that is exempt from obeying rules that common folks are expected to obey. This sense of entitlement and self-importance is pervasive among members of the print and broadcast news media. Since the reporter in question was also a bit pudgy and vertically challenged, I suppose that trying to intimidate a police officer who was taller and more fit made him feel better.

About two years before that incident, I was working in the detective bureau on a Monday morning when I received a phone call from a local newspaper reporter. He asked me about a vehicle pursuit that supposedly occurred during the weekend involving several of our officers. I told him that I did not normally work on weekends and that I was not aware of any such pursuit. He insisted that there was. I told him I would check with dispatch. I put him on hold and I asked the dispatcher if there was a pursuit over the weekend. She checked the radio and dispatch log and told me that there was no record of any pursuit involving any of our officers that weekend. I reconnected with the reporter and told him there was no record of any pursuit. He told me that he had a reliable source who told him about the pursuit. He accused me of lying to cover for the officers who were involved. I didn't like starting my day having my personal character and professional integrity called into question by a man who was little more than a glorified rumor monger, so I politely told him that he should speak with the chief about it and I terminated the call. He called the chief and asked about the alleged pursuit. The chief did the same thing I did and got the same results. When he told the reporter that there was no record of a pursuit, the reporter accused the chief of lying and covering for the officer. The chief terminated the call, but was annoyed enough to make some further inquiries. It turned out that several of our off duty officers were socializing together on Saturday night. They drove by one of their on duty coworkers who did not recognize their car. They thought it would be fun to bait him by turning off their headlights and speeding up. When they did, the on duty officer thought they were fleeing. He lit them up and called on the radio that he was in pursuit as they pulled into a convenience store parking lot. In less than five seconds, they stepped out with smiles on their faces. When the on duty officer recognized them and realized they had done, he told the dispatcher to cancel the pursuit call and to disregard it. The duration of the event was so brief that the dispatcher didn't have time to log it into the computer system before the officer canceled it. But the clerk at the convenience store where the officers pulled in did not like police officers and was also a friend of the reporter. The worst thing that could be said about the off duty officers' behavior was that it was childish. But there was no pursuit. Based only on inaccurate information supplied by a convenience store clerk who did not like police, the reporter jumped to a wrong conclusion and wanted to create a news story where there wasn't one. When the chief finally got to the bottom of it, he called the officers into his office and personally upbraided them for their childish behavior. But they did nothing worthy of any disciplinary action. There was no pursuit, no computer entry, and no attempt to cover anything up as presumed by the reporter.

UNSPORTSMANLIKE CONDUCT

Some professional sports celebrities play from the same page of music that the movie and television celebrities and news journalists play from. They take a knee on the field or on the court to show their support for criminals who are injured or killed by police. I suppose that should come as no surprise since many sports celebrities have their own histories of criminal behavior or confrontations with police officers. Some of those sports celebrities are just ignorant thugs who parlayed their natural genetic gifts and their unnatural lust for violence into multi-million dollar careers that depend upon both. In spite of their professional violence being regulated by rules and referees, they still can't control themselves. Let a referee, an umpire, an opposing player, a girlfriend, a spectator, or just about anyone else say or do something that rubs them the wrong way, and the professional athlete's default response is verbal threats or physical violence. So it should come as no surprise that the athletes who are predisposed to violence don't like cops who are legally responsible for preventing it. I won't waste space by including a list of the professional athletes who have been arrested for or been accused of violent or non-violent crimes. If you're that curious, you can do your own research.

If the sports celebrities who criticize us were cops, they wouldn't survive the affectionate insults we throw at each other during briefings, let alone the hate-filled rants that we patiently tolerate from the psychotic mutants we have to deal with in a typical tour of duty. I long ago quit watching "professional sports" because I saw enough violence and foolishness from criminals during my career. Watching sports celebrities being paid millions of dollars to be violent and foolish in stadiums and arenas isn't my idea of a good time. Professional athletes being arrested or having confrontations with police has become so commonplace that it is no longer considered embarrassing or shameful. It's viewed as rite of passage for which they can exchange high fives.

ARROGANCE IN ACADEMIA

Academic arrogance is the belief that having a degree in one field of endeavor automatically makes one an expert in other fields. (See the Dunning-Kruger Effect.) Here are just a few recent actual examples:

- A female professor of religion at one university attempted to organize a nationwide strike for academics against police violence.
- A male political scientist, who holds the Chair in Leadership at another university, lamented that academia had failed to improve police practices.
- Two male physicists at another university suggested that academic societies had a role in curbing police brutality.

Educated idiots, such as those in the above examples, are ubiquitous in modern educational institutions. They are educated beyond their intelligence. They are also a corrupting influence on the critical thinking skills of students who attend those institutions. These elitist professors seem to think the people we arrest are just nice folks who suffer from low self-esteem, and that those people would peacefully cooperate if we mean old cops would just give the thug a hug, a kind word and a ride home, instead of a "tune-up," a Miranda warning and a ride to jail. The reality is that most of the people we arrest are barely functional sociopaths who would put hot lead between our horns in a heartbeat if we gave them half a chance and if they thought they could get away with it. Some of them try. A few of them succeed. That's why we train to use deadly force and sometimes have to employ it. The elitist professors are horrified when we use deadly force. We'd like to see them load their intellectually illuminated carcasses into police cruisers for a few weeks and try to fulfill our statutory responsibilities without injuring or killing anyone. Watching them get beaten, stabbed, or shot to death in the process would be most entertaining.

Esoteric academic theories about how we should do our job might resonate impressively inside a university professor's empty skull while sipping latte in a professors' lounge or pontificating to gullible freshmen who are easily beguiled by linguistic gymnastics. But those theories make a dull thud when they hit the asphalt of the mean streets where we live and work.

Another example of professorial hubris was recently displayed in an exchange between a female professor and a nineteen year-old male student at a college in California. (California? Gee! What a surprise!) The student made some comments that were supportive of police, at one point referring to them as "heroes." The professor, a delusional forty year-old virago, bristled at that characterization.

Here are a few of her remarks: " . . the whole reason we have police departments in the first place, . . . it stems from people in the south wanting to capture runaway slaves."

I guess she didn't get the memo about the noble black lawmen who honorably served during the last half of the nineteenth and early twentieth centuries. Like the African-American police officers who were appointed to the police department in Selma, Alabama in 1867. And those appointed in Jacksonville, Florida in 1868, and in Houston and Galveston, Texas in 1870. And the more than one-hundred African-American officers in New Orleans, Louisiana in that same year. And Deputy U.S. Marshals like Bass Reeves, Rufus Cannon, and Bynum Colbert.)

She followed that asinine comment with the even more asinine: " . . police officers have committed atrocious crimes and have gotten away with it and have never been convicted of any of it."

Apparently she didn't get the other memo about the hundreds of officers nationwide who have been arrested, prosecuted, convicted and imprisoned for crimes. This woman is perhaps one of the stupidest people on the planet, but she's a college professor. She didn't name any officers or incidents to support her allegation, probably because she couldn't think of any. Evidently she also thinks cops are not entitled to the same constitutional protections that everyone else is entitled to. Protections like the right to due process; the right to a trial before a jury of their peers; the right to produce evidence and witnesses in their own defense; and the right to be considered innocent until proven guilty beyond a reasonable doubt in a court of law.

Prosecutors won't hesitate for a moment to charge cops with crimes if they think there is enough evidence to get a conviction. Occasionally a politically ambitious prosecutor will criminally charge an officer, not because there is enough evidence to convict the officer, but to score political points with angry protesters who have already decided the officer's guilt based on emotions rather than facts. Those trials are kangaroo courts, not legitimate judicial proceedings. The earlier described incident of the officer who shot the fleeing motorcyclist was one such case. I purposely saved a few of the details of that case to insert them here.

The state attorney of that judicial circuit was a liberal democrat who three years later was given a substantial political reward by a politically powerful sexual predator and pathological liar. Her office charged the officer with manslaughter. His attorney motioned for a change of venue. The state objected. The judge ruled in the state's favor, even though it should have been obvious to him that an appeals court would overturn his ruling. The excessive daily attention that the "if it bleeds, it leads" news media gave to the shooting exacerbated three days of riots that forced the closing of schools, the disruption of businesses, the rerouting of traffic, and a major inconvenience for many members of the community. It was impossible for the officer to get a fair trial before an impartial jury in that venue. Over objections by the officer's attorney, the judge also allowed the state to introduce into evidence the policy manual from the officer's agency. You don't have to be a lawyer to understand that juries in criminal cases must reach their verdict based upon evidence that the accused committed specific acts identified as elements of the crime as describe in state statutes. Agency policies are not state statutes. So why did the state attorney want to introduce the policy manual? To bolster what she knew was a statutorily weak criminal case by poisoning the minds of jurors who were duty bound to base their verdict on the statute alone. The officer was convicted. His attorney appealed. The appeals court vacated the verdict. A new trial was held in another venue two hundred miles away and the policy manual was excluded from the state's evidence. The officer was acquitted.

If the California professor had made her allegations about specific officers who had not been convicted in criminal or civil forums, her comments would have been slanderous and defamatory. She could have been sued. If you wonder how someone that stupid could be a college or university professor, wonder no more. When her comments went viral and she was mocked and criticized for making them, her colleagues responded by circling the wagons in her defense. In one pubic statement they said that they, ". . .stand in solidarity with all our faculty in protecting their academic freedom and the right to a safe work environment, free of hostility and threats to their physical safety and emotional well-being." The district's full-time faculty union said in a statement, "We request a strong and clear public statement in support of all faculty, and their right to a safe workspace and their ability to exercise their academic freedom."

Academic freedom does not give college and university professors a right to spew their subjective personal opinions and hostilities as objective facts without being publicly challenged by students. Professors who are so craven that they consider any challenge to their personal opinion to be a threat to their "physical safety and emotional well-being" should find another line of employment. Perhaps something in the child daycare industry where the most serious threats they would have to face are from small children who soil themselves.

If you're a student attending any university or college, don't leave your brain outside the door when you walk into the classroom. You're going to need it. And if professors publicly express their subjective personal opinions as facts, don't be afraid to publicly challenge them. If they feel threatened by your challenge, tell them to confine their comments to the course syllabus and to keep their personal opinions on unrelated topics to themselves.

Another incredibly stupid remark the professor made was something to the effect that she wouldn't call the police at all because she thinks her life would actually be in greater danger if placed in the hands of a police officer rather than those of a gun-wielding criminal. Having seen the professor's picture, I doubt that she will ever have to make that choice. But if a mother with two small children has to make that choice at two o'clock in the morning because her husband is two hundred miles away on business, and a six foot four inch, two hundred and fifty pound naked man with a butcher knife and a hard-on is trying to bash her door off the hinges, I'm going to guess that she will call 911 and take her chances with the cops. And when she does call 911, the phone won't ring at a university professors home. It will ring at a police dispatch center. And it won't be a university professor who is dispatched to save the woman and her children. It will be a trained law enforcement professional whose oath of office and code of ethics demands that he do whatever it takes to protect them. Do you think that mother, her children, and her husband want a university professor to show up to engage a knife wielding mad man in a philosophical debate? Or do you think they might prefer a man with a badge, a gun, an adrenaline honed edge, and the grit to stop at nothing to protect their lives, even at the risk of his own?

SOCIAL JUSTICE WARRIORS AND FRAUDS

When duty requires us to become physically aggressive with uncooperative suspects, social justice warriors (SJW's) are drawn to the event like flies are drawn to dung. A list of modern SJW's looks more like a membership roster of The Karl Marx Fan Club or a Who's Who Directory of Heretic Theologians. You won't see these warriors applying for the job when a law enforcement officer opening is posted on a city or county bulletin board. That's because they could not pass the police academy, the state certification exam, the civil service exam, the drug test, the physical exam, the psychological evaluation, the background investigation, the polygraph, and the oral interview that most of us had to pass to be hired as cops. SJW's who masquerade as "Christian Reverends" are particularly obnoxious since nothing they say or do bears any resemblance to anything taught or practiced by Christ and his Apostles. The reverend warriors claim to pray and fast for justice and peace. But I've never heard any of them utter anything that sounded even remotely like a Christian prayer. And, since most of those reverends could be poster children for an anti-obesity campaign, fasting is obviously not among their spiritual disciplines. They are wolves in sheep's clothing. They condemn us for enforcing laws that are based upon the precepts in the Bible that they fraudulently claim to believe in and selectively quote from, out of context. They use emotionally manipulative oratory to fleece their followers in order to pay for lavish lifestyles, adulterous mistresses and bastard children. Even worse, they prey upon the grief of people whose loved ones are killed while committing crimes or resisting police. They tell those mourners that the departed loved one is in heaven. It's hard to imagine a more cruel lie than telling a grieving person that their loved one, who lived an unrepentant life of chronic rebellion against God and crimes against their fellow man, and who died while resisting the police, will be rewarded with heavenly peace. If these so-called reverends truly believed the bible and cared about men and women whose hell-bound condition is demonstrated by criminal lives and violent deaths, those reverends would be setting virtuous examples and preaching the life-transforming gospel with the same zeal that they campaigned for our damnation. If they did, we'd probably go out of business for lack of people to arrest.

THE APPLE DOESN'T FALL FAR
FROM THE TREE

The foul-mouthed substance-abusing offspring of our critics have become the ignorant foot soldiers in the war that our critics wage against us. Unable to have an original thought of their own, or function outside of a mob, or abide by the most benign laws of a civilized society, those offspring blame their disastrous lives on everyone but themselves. And their parents support them by giving them shelter, posting their bail, paying their lawyers, and validating their excuses. When those offspring inevitably turn their antisocial belligerence against their parents, those parents call 911 for help. But when we arrive, mommy and daddy don't want us to arrest their little snowflake. They just want us to "talk to them" to try to get them to "be nice." We often try. But a few minutes of compassionate counseling by a wise veteran officer can't repair the decades of emotional, psychological, and spiritual damage done by horrible parents who were terrible role models.

WHAT A JOB!

Yes, cops put up with the ignorant insults of critics who don't have a clue about what our responsibilities are, or the difficulties of fulfilling those responsibilities within the framework of our legal system. The critics quake in fear at the societal savagery that they created, and then they expect us to tame that savagery with stoic equanimity. They think we're corrupt if we accept a free cup of coffee from an appreciative convenience store clerk at two in the morning. But they think they're exercising a constitutional right to pursue happiness when they drive drunk, sell drugs, abuse children, solicit prostitutes, or violate any other laws that interfere with their own moral bankruptcy. Eventually some of them will be caught and arrested. Some of them will resist arrest and get a trip to the emergency room for their trouble. A foolish few will escalate their resistance to a level of violence that will buy them a one-way ticket to Hell. Those who surrender peacefully will be treated with as much gentleness and respect as reasonable caution allows. In spite of that, they'll falsely accuse us of brutality, and then perjure themselves in court just to avoid a small fine or a few days in jail, both of which would do them a world of good.

Here is another truth that critics don't understand. We're not public safety officers. We're law enforcement officers. Public safety is the natural fruit of aggressive law enforcement. It's not our job to make people happy. It's our job to make them as safe as their legislators, jurists, and the constitution will allow us to. We're not the public's pal, priest, or shrink. We have no legal obligation to counsel wayward children, remove wild critters from homes, mediate infantile domestic arguments, resolve selfish civil disputes, or do any of the other things that our critics mistakenly think we are obliged to do to save them from the consequences of their own wanton foolishness. We provide those extra services freely because we care more about the welfare of the people we protect than our critics think we do. Certainly more than they care about ours. We certainly don't do it for the money. The critics also refuse to accept the reality that no one, regardless of age, sex, race, ethnicity, IQ, mental illness, social status, or opinion to the contrary, has a reasonable legal expectation that they can physically resist or assault us in the lawful performance of our duty without creating the possibility of being injured or killed in the process.

I'm not trying to excuse bad behavior by a tiny minority of cops. I'm only pointing out that our critics don't have the training, the experience, or the intelligence to understand the fine line between bad behavior and sound police tactics. Sure, we make occasional mistakes. It's easy for critics to condemn us for those mistakes when they can spend weeks analyzing them in the comfort and safety of their homes or offices. What they conveniently forget is that we probably made the mistake with only a split second to consider a few of the facts under circumstances that were gut-wrenching enough to make critics have a spontaneous bowel movement.

If you're a cop critic, do us a favor. The next time some feral two-legged predator selects you as their prey, don't call 911. Call the Screen Actors' Guild, the Associated Press, National Public Radio, CNN, ABC, NBC, CBS, The New York Times, The Los Angeles Times, the NFL, the NBA, Harvard, Yale, the Democratic National Committee, the American Civil Liberties Union, The White House, The US Congress, The FBI, The CIA, etc. and see how fast one of their witless demigods shows up to knowingly thrust his life between you and the grim reaper.

Being a cop is not a movie or a video game. It's a hellishly dangerous way to make a living. When things go bad for us, they go bad in a fraction of a single second; not in slow motion. There is no orchestra playing an award winning musical score in the background. We don't have time for a detailed critical analysis of the potential ramifications of every possible option. We don't have a pause or reset button we can push to get more time or start over. And there is no algorithmic flow chart that gives us a pain-free sure-fire solution to every problem we encounter. Sometimes things happen so rapidly and unexpectedly that we have to make instant decisions based on raw instinct and reflex. Our daily work environment is hostile and unpredictable enough to keep us painfully aware of our human shortcomings without being reminded of them by spineless blowhards.

Since you critics don't know the physical and psychological price cops pay for a twenty-plus-year career on the streets, consider this: A troubling percentage of those cops will die from a massive heart attack, a stroke, cancer, or some other stress induced illness within a few short years after retirement if they don't die sooner from a self-inflicted gunshot wound to the head. Until then, they suffer with varying degrees of chronic physical pain from on-the-job injuries sustained in fights, foot pursuits, and traffic crashes. They have chronic insomnia from circadian clocks that were destroyed by decades of rotating shifts. And, when they can sleep, it isn't unusual for them to be awakened by nightmares generated by PTSD from years of verbal and physical confrontations with the most depraved people that a terminally toxic society can produce. You critics should thank God that He sent your flawed fellow human beings to enforce your laws. If He had sent His angels to enforce them, most of you would have been incinerated before you reached the end of my opening sentence.

We don't expect your sympathy, and we long ago gave up any hope of having your respect. We'd be satisfied if you would just shut up and stay out of our way. It would be better still if you spent your time and energy obeying the law and being good role models for the inordinate number of people who foolishly think you are worthy of their admiration. The effort would prove so time consuming and exhausting that you wouldn't have any time or energy left to criticize us.

LAW ENFORCEMENT 101

This section is for non-critics who might be confused from watching too many movies and television shows about fictional cops, or from seeing too many news stories about incidents that real cops are involved in. The news stories are deceptively lopsided. The movies and television shows have as much to do with the realities of law enforcement as "Star Trek" has to do with Sputnik. And the phrase "To protect and to serve," is as ambiguous as, "To boldly go where no man has gone before." Seeing "To protect and to serve" on the side of a police vehicle might give people a warm fuzzy feeling, but it is not our job; at least not in the sense that people understand the phrase. It isn't even a job description. It's a commercial jingle that was created to give goose bumps to people who have been conditioned to evaluate reality and truth by their emotional responses rather than by objective facts and logic. I'm not aware of any law enforcement oath of office that says anything about ". . . protect and serve."

The oaths that I took during my career all contained a phrase along the line of: "I do solemnly swear that I will support, protect, and defend the Constitution of the Government of the United States and of the State of Florida, against all enemies, foreign and domestic (etc.) . . . . So help me God."

Did you notice that the oath does not say anything about protecting and serving people? That's because people are best protected and served when officers diligently support, protect, and defend the Constitution. The concept of protecting people is more specifically contained in state statues, in our code of ethics, and in our policy and procedure manuals. It is ironic that cops often get blamed for the societal problems that are created by the politicians and lawyers who make the rules that cops have to play by. Those politicians and lawyers have the financial wherewithal to insulate themselves from the painful consequences of those rules. Laws, legal interpretations, and plea deals hammered out by these highly educated political and legal philosophers have filled the public highways and byways with people whose moral degeneracy is beyond the capacity of the average law abiding citizen to fully comprehend. As a result, cops often find themselves burdened with the challenge of protecting the lives and property of law abiding citizens on one hand, while on the other hand protecting the legal rights of recidivist criminals who are little more than wild beasts. Those laws, legal interpretations, and plea deals allow career criminals to remain free to harm the citizens we're supposed to protect.

A normal law abiding person who has a momentary lapse of judgment that lands him (or her) in jail usually finds the experience unpleasant enough to make them avoid doing something in the future that will send them back again. People with criminal dispositions don't mind going to jail. It's only a momentary inconvenience. Many of them have so many frequent flier miles in the system that they are on a first name basis with the corrections staff and the other inmates at those facilities. For them, going to jail isn't an unpleasant punishment. It's a reunion with old friends or family members, free meals, a bed to sleep in, and free medical and dental care. Don't assume that those criminals are mentally ill or intellectually challenged. Some of them are downright brilliant. Haven't you ever wondered why, if prisons are such terrible places, the same people keep going back to them? They understand the risks to themselves and the pain to others that their criminal behavior causes. They just don't care. They place their own immediate carnal or material gratification above the welfare of every other living creature. Critics don't have to interact with them, at least not at the same level of intimacy and frequency that cops do. And that is up close and personal, every day.

Critics want to replace cops and jails with psychologists and mental health clinics. Psychologists and mental health clinics do not protect law abiding people from harm. I am not opposed to mental health counseling. But the mental health community grossly over estimates its own ability to influence the thinking and behavior of people who have criminal dispositions. Cops aren't psychologists or social workers. But that doesn't mean we enjoy harming the people we arrest. Many of us have our own dysfunctional family histories and personal demons to battle. While those histories and demons give us the capacity to feel some level of empathy towards some of the troubled souls that we have to arrest, that doesn't mean we can ignore their crimes, or that we won't defend ourselves from them when they decide to physically resist or assault us.

NOT OUR CIRCUS, NOT OUR MONKEYS

You might be surprised to learn that a significant amount of law enforcement time, energy and resources are wasted on complaints that have nothing to do with law enforcement. A troubling percentage of those complaints are about barking dogs, loud parties, wild critters in homes, disobedient children, landlord / tenant disputes, civil disputes about money owed or services rendered, etc. Here are few anecdotes to illustrate the point.

One morning I was dispatched to an apartment complex because a woman called 911 to complain that her fifteen year-old son refused to go to school. When I arrived, I was greeted by the complainant; a morbidly obese 33 year-old white single mother wearing shorts, flip-flops, an ill-fitting t-shirt and no bra. She was sporting multiple tattoos, a cigarette in one hand and a beer in the other. I had her wait outside so I could talk to her son privately inside. He was vibrating from emotional distress. He hated his mother and had no father figure to talk to. So I gave him some fatherly advice that calmed him down. When he considered the logic of my advice, he decided to go to school and he asked me for a ride. I was glad to take him. I also gave him a business card and told him that he could call me in the future if he needed advice or just needed to talk to a man.

Another afternoon I was dispatched to a complaint from a man who said there was a snake in his house. When I arrived, the terrified forty year-old black male home owner was standing on his kitchen table. He said that he lost sight of the snake and he asked me to come in and find it. I located a three foot Eastern Diamondback rattlesnake in his living room. I chopped its head off with a butcher knife from the kitchen. I put the snake in a plastic bag and secured the bag in the trunk of my cruiser. Then I looked around the outside of the man's house to try to find how the snake got in. I found a three inch hole in the block wall about a foot above the ground. The hole had been there for a several years and was clearly the snake's point of entry. The man was aware of the hole. He was just too lazy to fix it. It would have taken him about two dollars' worth of material and ten minutes of his time.

On another occasion I was dispatched to a domestic complaint at an apartment complex. I contacted the white male complainant at his apartment. His complaint was that his boyfriend habitually stayed out late to party, and then wouldn't have sex with him when he got home. I told him that there was nothing I could do about it. I suggested that he get some professional psychiatric counseling.

They don't show you calls like those in movies, television shows, or news broadcasts because violence and bloodshed are much more interesting. But calls like those consume more of a cops time than you realize. Those complaints rob citizens of legitimate law enforcement services. Cops are supposed to be preventing and solving crimes, enforcing traffic laws, and putting bad guys in jail; not counseling the damaged children of destructive parents, or removing vipers from the homes of irresponsible home owners, or intervening in the domestic relationships of sexual deviants. Perhaps explaining it in the following terms will help you better understand.

The laws of your state are written and passed by legislators that you elect. Most of those laws are based on public safety concerns that citizens express to their legislators. Some laws are regulatory and have to do with the standards and practices of private businesses and government agencies. For example: Restaurants and physical therapy providers have to comply with certain health and safety regulations. The government agencies that license those businesses are responsible for making sure that those businesses are in compliance with those regulations, and issuing them civil citations if they are not. Those regulations are usually listed in non-criminal statutes, state administrative codes, municipal or county ordinances, and are usually enforced by regulatory or code enforcement officers. Legislators also pass criminal laws that are designed to protect lives and property from evil doers. The personnel who enforce those laws are called law enforcement officers, aka "Cops." Because of the immediate physical or financial harm that can be done by people who violate those laws, state constitutions and legislatures grant law enforcement officers the power to seize (arrest) people to stop the harmful activity, to seize evidence, and to bring the offender before some magisterial authority, by force if necessary. Since some of those people violently resist, officers are authorized to carry an assortment of weapons, including firearms, and to use those weapons if it becomes necessary to carry out their duties. Law abiding citizens expect cops to carry out those duties in spite of resistance from the offender. We don't stop or arrest people because we're bored or lonely. We stop or arrest them when they do something that gives us reasonable suspicion that they committed or are about to commit some crime or civil infraction, or when someone calls 911 to report some criminal or suspicious act is afoot. An officer who arrests someone must meticulously document what that person did and the statutory elements of the crime for which the person is arrested. The arrested person's loss of liberty is only temporary, and the arresting officer has no control over it once the person is booked at the jail. Except in unusual circumstances, the arrested person will be released on their own recognizance or can bond out of jail. If they hire an attorney to fight the charge, the officer might not see them again until trial. Sometimes a state attorney chooses not to prosecute an arrested person. That does not mean the arresting officer did something wrong. What it probably means is that the state attorney is so swamped with cases that it is physically impossible to prosecute every arrested person. There are simply not enough prosecutors, judges, juries, or courtrooms available to try everyone who is arrested. And there isn't enough prison space to house the people who would be convicted. So it becomes necessary for the state attorney to prioritize cases according to the seriousness of the offense and the history of the offender. Cops and prosecutors use different standards in their official functions. Cops stop people based on reasonable suspicion, and arrest them based on probable cause. Reasonable suspicion means that the person did something that gives the officer a reason to suspect that a crime might have been committed, or is about to be committed. Probable cause means there is concrete evidence of a crime, and that the person arrested committed that crime. Probable cause requires that officers have more than just suspicion, but not to the extent of absolute certainty or proof beyond a reasonable doubt. Prosecutors must be able to prove, in court, before a judge or jury, that a person is guilty beyond a reasonable doubt. A prosecutor can be confident that the arresting officer had enough probable cause to arrest someone. But that prosecutor might not be confident that he can prove in court that the arrested person is guilty beyond a reasonable doubt. So the case is dropped and the arrested person is released. Since most of the people officers arrest can be proven guilty beyond a reasonable doubt, the sheer volume of cases sometimes forces prosecutors to drop less serious cases or to offer sweet plea deals to entice the offender to plead guilty to a lesser crime and accept probation just to make room for more serious cases to be taken to trial. So the bad guys just keep going through the revolving doors of the criminal justice system, the public continues to be victimized, and the police continue to be blamed.

Our critics want you to believe that, when we're not brutally beating cooperative innocent people for fun, we're just sitting around drinking coffee and eating donuts. Several decades ago I was working day shift as a deputy sheriff. I stopped for a coffee break at a popular national donut franchise. As I sipped my coffee and stuffed a donut down my gullet, an elderly gent stopped at my table for a moment as he headed for the door. He asked me what my yearly salary was. Since it was a matter of public record, I didn't mind telling him. He smiled and said, "Wow. They pay you all that just to drink coffee and eat donuts?" He wasn't trying to be obnoxious. It was just his awkward attempt to be sociable.

So I smiled back and replied, "No. I drink coffee and eat donuts for free. They pay me all that for the one fraction of second during the year when a bullet strikes the shock plate in my ballistic vest because some cop hating psycho wasn't a good enough shot to hit me in the head." His smile disappeared for a moment as he processed my reply. Then he smiled a bit, shook his head, wished me a good day and headed for the door. For those of you who think my reply was bit melodramatic, here is a fictional but entirely plausible scenario for you to think about. And, since accusations of racism figure so prominently in so much of the criticism we're subjected to, I'll include a racial dynamic in the scenario.

Imagine that you're a white male police officer working the 6 P.M. to 6 A.M. shift. It's 2 A.M. on a clear, fifty degree Sunday morning. The officer assigned to the zone beside yours is dispatched to an alarm at an electronics retail store. You head that way as a backup officer. The primary officer arrives almost immediately. He radios that the front window is broken out and the laptop computer display was knocked over, but there is no one inside the store. When you're five blocks from the store, you see a tall athletic black male suspect wearing a sweat suit, sneakers, and carrying a laptop computer. He is approximately twenty-five years old. He is walking in the opposite direction from the store. He is breathing heavily and is sweating. You advise dispatch of your location and you order the suspect to stop. Unfortunately for you, there is not another officer available to back you up. The suspect stops. You ask him if he has any identification. He says he does not. You ask him his name and date of birth. He tells you his name is John Smith and he gives you a date of birth that makes him twenty-five years old. You ask him where he is coming from and where he is going. He tells you that he just left his house. He tells you that he bought the computer yesterday as a birthday gift for a friend and was taking it to that friend when you stopped him. Not convinced by his story, you advise him of his rights per Miranda vs Arizona before you question him further. He immediately invokes his rights and calls you a racist mother fucker. He says that he has done nothing wrong and that you're just harassing him because he is black. He demands that you allow him to be on his way without any further delay. You now have two options, each of which creates a host of other potential problems. Option one is cuff him and secure him in your car. Option two is let him go. Well? What are you going to do? Release him and allow him to disappear into the darkness with the computer? Or are you going to arrest him? Do you think his story is credible? Even if you don't, is there a possibility that it is the truth? Do you think you have probable cause to arrest him? If so, for what? If you do arrest him, do you think a prosecutor can prove him guilty beyond a reasonable doubt in court based only on what you know if the computer manufacturer and the store owner cannot produce records that prove the computer is from the store's inventory? What if his story is true?

This is just an exercise for you to think about, so I'm not going to tell you what to do. But I will tell you the possible results of either decision you make, and you'd better pray that your body camera is turned on and working properly. If you let him go, you'll never see him or the computer again. The store owner who depended upon you for the safety of his business and property will be another victim statistic. Since the personal information the suspect gave you is false, and he actually lives two hundred miles away, you won't be able to track him down or figure out who he is. If you try to arrest him, he's going to run. If your reflexes are fast enough to reach out and grab him before he gets away, and if you're strong enough to hold on to him, you're going to have a serious fight on your hands. If he does get away and you chase him, you won't catch him because you're wearing duty boots and fifteen pounds of duty gear. He's carrying a four-pound laptop and wearing sweats and Nikes. During the chase, he might suddenly turn and shoot you with the gun that was hidden in his pants. If he isn't armed, and if he is slow enough for you to catch him, you can be sure that he is going to fight like a tiger to get away from you. If he is stronger or a more skilled fighter than you are, he might injure you badly enough to render you temporarily or permanently unable to defend yourself. If he does, he might take your gun away from you. What then? What if he shoots and kills you? Who's going to take care of your wife and kids? If he just wounds you severely enough to permanently disable you, who's going to pay your bills when your employer terminates you because you can no longer do the job they hired you for? Who's going to take care of you when your attractive young wife divorces you because she doesn't have the grit to push you around in a wheel chair, spoon feed you, and wipe your backside for the rest of your life? ("But she promised for better or for worse!" You must be joking!) What if he doesn't shoot you? What if he just takes your gun and runs away? What if he shows up at an elementary school on Monday and kills fifteen children with the fifteen rounds that were in your pistol when he took it from you? What if he uses your gun to kill a brother officer? If you are strong and skilled enough to finally take him into custody, there's a high probability that the ferocity of his resistance is going to require that you use a level of force that will cause visible injuries such as cuts, broken bones and missing teeth. If he doesn't need to be hospitalized, he'll at least need to be taken to the emergency room to be medically cleared by a doctor before the jail will accept him. What are you going to do when he gets out of the hospital or bonds out of jail and files a complaint with your employer, the FBI, and the NAACP accusing you of committing a hate crime and violating his constitutional rights by brutally beating him for no reason while you were calling him the dreaded "N" word? How are you going to feel when you're put on administrative leave while internal affairs investigates his false allegations? How are you going to feel when you turn on the evening news and see video of an angry mob of protesters in front of city hall calling for you to be fired and prosecuted for police brutality? How are you going to feel when you change the channel and see some Hollywood celebrity implicitly referring to you and saying, "Something needs to be done about systemic racism and police brutality!" How are you going to feel when you turn the channel again to watch a ball game and you see half of the players on your favorite team kneeling in honor of the guy who tried to beat your brains out and who is falsely accusing you of racism and brutality? How are you going to feel when FBI agents show up at your home, read your Miranda rights to you, and then want to question you about the civil rights violation allegation? How are you going to feel when you invoke your rights, tell the FBI agents to pound sand, and five minutes later get a phone call from your boss ordering you to cooperate with them or face disciplinary action? Does all of that sound far-fetched to you? Well, it isn't. All I did was stitch together bits and pieces from actual events that have happened to real officers.

Here's another scenario for you to think about. This one has no meaningful racial dynamic. You're Officer Bobby Smith, a seasoned black male police officer. You're on patrol at 8am on a Tuesday morning when you see a car fail to come to a complete stop at a stop sign in a school zone. So you conduct a traffic stop. The driver is Mr. Jones, a local white business man. You approach Jones and say "Good morning. I'm officer Smith of the Police Department. May I see your driver's license, registration and insurance, please?" Instead of complying with your request, Jones indignantly replies, "Why did you stop me?!" While you are not legally required give Jones an explanation before he is required to produce the requested documents, you offer an explanation as a courtesy. The downside to that is that some drivers ask the question to distract the officer and to buy time to come up with the name of a friend or relative and a ruse to explain why they don't have a license with them; or to come up with a gun to shoot the momentarily distracted officer. Other drivers view an explanation as an invitation to argue about whether or not they committed the violation.

The Florida legislature no doubt understood that would happen when they wrote Florida Statute 322.15 which states in part: "Every licensee shall have his or her driver license. . . in his or her immediate possession at all times when operating a motor vehicle and shall present or submit the same upon the demand of a law enforcement officer. . ."

Did you notice the words "upon demand?" That seems clear enough. If Jones can't produce a driver's license, but you can use other reliable means to verify that Jones has a valid license, you can issue him a separate citation for failure to carry and exhibit on demand.

But let's assume the disgruntled Mr. Jones produces a license and you issue him a citation for running the stop sign. That ends the encounter, right? Not so fast! Jones still has to sign the citation. So you explain the citation and ask Jones to sign it. Jones refuses. You explain that signing the citation is not an admission of guilt. It's only an acknowledgment that Jones is receiving a copy of the citation and is promising to comply with one of his options, which are:

1. Plead guilty and pay a fine.
2. Complete a driver improvement course.
3. Request a court date to contest the charge.

In spite of that, Jones continues to refuse to sign the citation. You explain that refusing to sign the citation is a criminal violation for which Jones will be arrested. Jones still refuses to sign it. When you say. "Okay. You're under arrest." and you put your hands on Jones to effect the arrest, Jones physically resists. Let's assume Jones is a lightweight and that you can cuff him and put him into the back seat of your cruiser without either of you being injured.

Now, in addition to the civil citation for running the stop sign, Jones will be criminally charged with violating Florida Statute 318.14(3) which states: "Any person who willfully refuses to accept and sign a summons as provided in subsection (2) commits a misdemeanor of the second degree." He will also be charged with violating Florida Statute 843.02 which states: "Whoever shall resist, obstruct, or oppose any officer. . . legally authorized to execute process. . . without offering or doing violence to the person of the officer, shall be guilty of a misdemeanor of the first degree. . ."

As he sits in the back seat of your cruiser, the gravity of his foolish decision begins to dawn on him and he says, "Okay! Okay! I'll sign the citation!" Too late. Next stop, the county jail. But you still have to deal with

Jones' vehicle which is stopped partially on the roadway. You can have it towed or, if Jones requests, you can try to contact a licensed driver that Jones authorizes to come and take possession of the vehicle if they can do so in a reasonable amount of time.

Let's assume that you have the vehicle towed. You must document the vehicle's contents and condition on a towing report before the towing company's driver will remove the vehicle. This is a lawful procedure to protect officers and towing companies from accusations that a vehicle was damaged or that items were stolen from it after it was towed. This is classified as an inventory, not a search. However, if contraband or evidence of a crime is found during the inventory, you can impound that contraband or evidence, charge Jones with possession of it, and it can be used as evidence in court. But let's say that no contraband is found. In addition to the citation and towing report, you will have to fill out a probable cause affidavit, an incident report, and a use of force report. So, while you were tied up completing all of the paperwork related to Jones' idiocy, a car was stolen, a house was burglarized, and a convenience store was robbed in your zone. The victims of those crimes are unhappy because they assume you were stuffing your face with donuts instead of protecting them and their property. If cops didn't have to waste time on problems created by idiots like Jones, they could spend more time deterring and solving crimes on behalf of good citizens.

Let's assume that Jones doesn't resist, isn't injured, and that you can contact Jones' wife to come for the vehicle. When Mrs. Jones arrives, she sees Mr. Jones in the back seat of your cruiser. When you explain the circumstances, Mrs. Jones demands that you release Mr. Jones and allow him to sign the citation. You refuse. You release the car to Mrs. Jones who angrily drives it away. Oh, and by the way; if you forgot to verify that Mrs. Jones has a valid driver's license and she does not, and if she strikes and kills a pedestrian at the next intersection, guess who is going to be held civilly responsible. That's right. You are, because you allowed someone with no license or a suspended license to drive the car from the scene; the car that you were responsible for. Fortunately she has a valid license and doesn't kill anyone when she leaves. After you deliver Jones to the county jail and complete the related paperwork, you resume your patrol duties. Jones will be processed and allowed to bond out of jail or released on his own recognizance. Jones' wife picks him up at the jail.

So the contentious Mr. Jones has turned a simple traffic stop for a minor traffic infraction into a criminal arrest. Mr. and Mrs. Jones now hate the police and spread their lopsided version of the events to all of their friends and neighbors who assume the account is true and join the "we hate the police" parade. Jones and his wife also complain to their good friend who happens to be the mayor. The mayor then calls the police chief and demands an explanation as to why Jones was arrested instead of released with a citation. The chief will ask you about the event and will back you up after you explain the details. But it's still just one more administrative aggravation that he has to deal with.

Let's go back to the point at which Jones resisted arrest. Let's assume that Jones is bigger, stronger, and a more skilled fighter than you are, and that his resistance is violent. At some point during this battle you realize that Jones will seriously injure or kill you if the fight continues another five seconds. You must choose between several possible use of force options that must quickly be acted upon, and your life or death could hinge on you making the right choice. The clock is ticking.

1. Impact weapon. (straight or expandable baton)
2. Chemical agent. (pepper spray)
3. Electronic control device. (taser)
4. Lethal force. (firearm)

Let's look at each of those options individually and consider some of the problems with each.

1. **Impact weapons:** In order to subdue a violent or aggressive person by striking them with an impact weapon, such as a baton, the aim and the amount of force behind the weapon must be within narrow parameters. Too much force can cause serious injury. Not enough force will only motivate the person to resist harder and make them more dangerous than they already are. There is no scientific chart or formula for how much force is required to subdue each person. Everyone's vulnerability is different, and you can't necessarily tell by looking at them. Their vulnerability can be influenced by size,

weight, physical fitness, combat training, pain threshold, drug influence, adrenaline, mental illness, medical conditions, officer strength and skill, etc. Furthermore, impact weapon strikes are supposed to be non-lethal force and are therefore restricted to certain parts of the body such as major muscle groups in the arms or legs. Striking someone on a part of their body, such as their head, face, neck, or genitals, could cause death or serious bodily injury and is automatically considered to be deadly force that is prohibited unless deadly force is justified. The location of those body parts in relation to where the officer intends to strike the person can change rapidly during a violent struggle. So an officer who takes a righteous and appropriately forceful swing at a resisting suspect's deltoid muscle could fracture the suspect's skull if the suspect suddenly dips his head to where his deltoid was a fraction of a second earlier. Expecting an officer to see, process, and respond to all of these factors and the sudden change a split second before impact is unrealistic.

2. **Chemical agents:** Like the baton, chemical agents, such as pepper spray, are valuable tools. But, like the baton, the conditions under which chemical agents are effective are subject to some of the same factors as the baton. In addition to those factors are wind direction, wind speed, distance from the intended target, and proximity to innocent bystanders. Critics expect officers to be able to accurately calculate all of those factors before deploying the agent, in spite of some of those factors being beyond the officers ability to anticipate because they are subject to change without warning. Officers who deploy chemical agents against suspects are often in such close proximity to the suspect that they suffer some level of exposure to the agent. If that exposure is severe enough, the officer could be partially impaired by it and become more vulnerable to the suspect than he was before he deployed the agent, especially if the suspect's physical or mental state makes him less vulnerable to it than the officer is. And if some of that chemical agent is caught by a sudden gust of wind and is carried into the eyes and nostrils of some innocent bystander, that

bystander will be calling a personal injury lawyer before the sun sets. Heaven knows there is no shortage of them advertising on television, radio, and roadside billboards.

3. **Electronic control devices:** An officer can shoot a suspect with a Taser, but that is no guarantee it will be effective. One or both probes might miss the target. One probe might fall out or be pulled out by the suspect. The Taser might malfunction. The suspect might be wearing clothing that prevents the Taser probes from penetrating enough to be effective. Or the suspect might be one of those rare individuals who isn't fully disabled and continues to resist, even after the Taser probes properly deploy and the electronic components function as they are supposed to.

4. **Deadly force:** Deadly force is, ". . . any force that is likely to cause serious bodily injury or death." Bare hands can be considered deadly force if they are used in a way that could reasonably be expected to cause serious bodily injury or death. But most people associate deadly force with the officer's firearm, and the firearm is usually the weapon of choice when deadly force is called for. I've heard critics say, "The officer should have fired a warning shot to give the suspect a chance to surrender!" Wrong. The suspect's chance to surrender was when the officer said, "You're under arrest," or "Stop!" or "Stop resisting!" Firing a warning shot rarely makes a suspect stop. It usually just makes them run faster or fight harder. Firing warning shots is against the policy of nearly all law enforcement agencies. When an officer fires his weapon, he is responsible for everything the bullet strikes between the time it leaves the barrel until it comes to rest. A bullet fired towards the ground can ricochet and hit who knows what. A bullet fired into the air will come down, who knows where. Here's another legal tidbit; If an officer discharges his firearm in someone's direction, even if the officer does not intend to strike the person, it is still considered deadly force. If deadly force was not justified, the officer could be criminally charged.

I've also heard critics complain, "The officer didn't have to kill him. He could have just winged him in the arm or leg!" Really? Like they do on TV and in the movies? That's absurd. Hitting a stationary paper target accurately and consistently at the range requires practice. Delivering an accurate shot under high stress onto the arm or leg of an uncooperative living human target is more challenging. If that human target is a moving one, it is much more difficult and takes nearly as much luck as it does skill. People who think cops should shoot resisting criminals in the arm or leg are ignorant of human anatomy and firearm ballistics. Bullets do not always travel in a straight trajectory through human tissue. A bullet that hits an arm or leg is likely to exit and continue to travel, possibly striking an innocent person. Or it could strike a bone or artery. There are major arteries in the arms and legs. Fatal damage to those arteries can be caused by a bullet or bone fragment. Causing damage to a major artery in an extremity could kill someone faster than a bullet that strikes them in the torso, but misses their vital organs. A bullet that hits someone in the torso is more likely to remain there and not exit and strike someone else. Critics also consider it unnecessarily brutal when an officer shoots someone multiple times. Being shot only one time rarely takes the fight out of a suspect who is running on adrenaline or on drugs. Gunshot wounds have a cumulative effect. That is why officers are trained to "double-tap." That means fire at least two rounds into the target. Officers do not shoot to kill. They shoot to stop violent aggression. There are numerous incidents where suspects have been mortally wounded by firearms, but did not fall down and die before being able to kill or injure another person or persons. Some people think officers should let suspects go rather than shoot them, even when deadly force is legally justified. Wrong again. Suspects should surrender peacefully rather than risk being shot. Cops have a statutory and ethical obligation to take criminals into custody. They are not supposed to retreat or relent from that obligation simply because the criminal offers resistance or flees. If a cop, who has legal justification to use deadly force against a criminal, allows the criminal to escape, and that criminal subsequently uses his liberty to harm an innocent person or persons, who do you think the public will hold responsible for that harm? The cop who allowed him to escape, of course.

You might ask, "What do these use of force issues have to do with a simple traffic stop?" The answer is that many of the violent confrontations cops are forced into are preceded by traffic stops. A driver who is uncooperative or verbally argumentative when stopped, or who flees when an officer tries to stop him, often becomes physically combative. Thus, a minor traffic infraction turns into a violent confrontation. As a law abiding citizen, you have a right to expect officers to carry out their duties, even when confronted with verbal or physical resistance. In a scenario where an officer has to choose between injuring or killing a traffic violator who decides to violently resist, or to allow the violator to injure or kill him, there is no winner. Only a survivor. Smart officers choose survival. This unpleasant choice could easily be avoided by simple polite cooperation on the part of the driver.

In the present scenario, let's go back to the point where you, Officer Smith, ask Jones to sign the citation. Jones grudgingly signs it, takes his copy and drives away. You continue with your patrol duties and don't think much more about the event. You don't care which citation option Jones chooses. But Jones drives from the stop and angrily stews over the citation for several days. He finally decides to schedule a court hearing to plead not guilty. A month later you receive a subpoena to testify against him in traffic court. Your shift has changed since you issued the citation. You are now on the 6 P.M. to 6 A.M shift. That means you will have to appear in court when you would normally have been sleeping. When Jones shows up in court, he is confident that he will prevail because it's his word against yours.

When the case is called, you tell the judge the date, the time, the location, and the details of the violation. Jones then presents his defense which consists of, "I stopped at the stop sign. Smith is lying."

After listening to your account of the violation and to Jones' defense, the judge tells Jones, "I find you guilty and I fine you $250.00 plus court costs, and I assess three points against your driver's license." Jones is infuriated, but he pays the fine. He leaves the courtroom convinced that you and the judge are drinking buddies who are in some kind of corrupt conspiracy to get rich by screwing good citizens out of their hard earned money. In reality, the only time you see or speak to the judge is on those occasions that you have to go to court. Those occasions are rare because most of the people that you cite have enough honesty to admit that they are guilty. So they pay the fine to avoid court. And, contrary to what Jones wrongly believes, you don't have to prove beyond a reasonable doubt that he ran the stop sign. Failing to stop at a stop sign is a civil infraction, not a criminal violation. The threshold in civil cases is not proof beyond a reasonable doubt. It's preponderance. The judge only has to be satisfied that your account of the event is more credible than Jones's. Jones thinks this is grossly unfair.

After all, "Why should the judge believe Smith more than me?" That's a fair question with a fair answer. The judge rightly assumes that you were carrying out your duties in a professional and unbiased manner. Absent any clear evidence or credible inference to the contrary, the judge is right in making that assumption, and you are entitled to the benefit of any speculative doubt. You don't get a commission on traffic fines for the citations you write. The most you might get out of it is a little overtime pay if you have to show up in court on your day off. And the amount of overtime paid isn't worth the aggravation of having to cancel your previous recreational plans just so you can make a court appearance. In this case, it isn't your day off. But you are off-duty. So you'll be paid a little overtime. That overtime doesn't compensate for the fact that you had to sit in court all morning waiting for Jones' case to be called. Now you won't get home and get into bed until 1 P.M. Since you have to be up at 5pm to get prepared and back at work at 6 P.M, you will have to work another twelve hour shift on four hours of sleep and will probably suffer diminished cognitive function due to fatigue. Since the judge is aware of issues like these, he has no reason to assume that your actions were anything other than professional. Jones on the other hand is motivated by a desire to avoid paying a fine and higher insurance premiums because of a conviction for a moving violation. Judges are not insensitive to the plight of a driver who receives a citation, but who has an otherwise good driving record. That's why judges sometimes withhold adjudication if the driver pleads "no contest" and offers an explanation of some extenuating circumstance. Officers aren't insensitive to the plight of those driver's either. Modern technology in many departments allows officers to access a driver's history on the computer in their cars during the traffic stop. Since officers have some discretionary latitude in issuing citations for civil traffic infractions, a polite and cooperative driver with a good driving record might leave the traffic stop with a verbal or written warning instead of a citation. An argumentative driver whose driving record demonstrates a chronic disregard for traffic laws is almost assured of getting a citation instead of a warning. Drivers in that latter group have a dark psychological compulsion to disregard the welfare of others and to defy lawful authority. That compulsion is frequently reflected in their criminal history as well as their driving history. They eventually get enough citations and accumulate enough points for the division of motor vehicles to suspend their driver's license. Does that stop them from driving? Of course not. They continue to drive while their license is suspended, and they continue to disregard traffic laws. It doesn't take long before they commit another violation in front of another officer.

Let's assume that Jones is one of those driver's and that he runs another stop sign. This time Officer Burns happens to witness the violation. Burns does not personally know Jones or know that Jones' license is suspended. So Burns lights him up. When Jones sees the blue lights in his mirror, he has a choice: To flee or not to flee; that is the question. Since Jones knows his license is suspended, and that driving on a suspended license is an arrestable offense, Jones decides to flee. As a seasoned officer, Burns knows that everyone who flees from the police does so for one or more of the following reasons:

- They have no driver's license.
- Their license is suspended.
- They are chemically impaired.
- They have illegal drugs, weapons, or stolen property in the vehicle.
- The vehicle is stolen.
- They are leaving the scene of a crime.
- They are in violation of their probation.
- There is a warrant for their arrest.

Now there is a high speed pursuit that endangers the lives of Burns, Jones, and whoever happens to be in the path of that pursuit. Jones loses control of his car and crashes into a utility pole. Jones is seriously injured and trapped in his car. The utility pole snaps. The power and phone service to nine hundred homes is knocked out, as well as power to three traffic signals. Several of the residents in the effected community are home-bound people with medical conditions that require the use of electrically powered medical devices for their survival. The emergency backup power supplies on those devices will fail before power is restored to those customers. So they have to be transported to the hospital or some alternate location by neighbors because the only available fire and emergency medical crews are busy trying to extract Jones from his mangled vehicle to save his life. The only other available officers are directing traffic at the intersections where the signals failed. Who do critics blame for these calamitous events? Officer Burns, of course. The critics think, "If Burns had not been chasing Jones, none of that would have happened. After all, the only thing Jones did was run a stop sign." The fact that Burns didn't know that at the time is irrelevant to the critics. Let's suppose that Jones had a clean driving record and a valid driver's license. But let's also suppose that he was an undiscovered pedophile and serial killer who had a small child bound and gagged in the trunk of his car. When he ran the stop sign, he was on his way to a remote area to rape and kill the child, and then bury the body in a shallow grave beside four of his other victims. But, as far as Burns knows, all Jones did was run a stop sign. Because of the inherent danger of high speed pursuits, and the potential civil liability to Burns, his supervisor and the department if Jones crashes or injures someone, Burns's supervisor orders him to terminate the pursuit. Burns breaks off the pursuit and Jones disappears into the distance. When the child's naked decomposing body is found, and evidence is found linking Jones to the crime on the date of the pursuit, the critics who condemned Burns for the pursuit in the previous scenario will blame him, his supervisor, and the department for the child's death in the second scenario because Burns did not pursue Jones to the gates of hell to save the child, in spite of Burns having no way of knowing that Jones was a serial killer or that a child was in the trunk of the car.

Are you starting to understand that what cops routinely do is far more complex than you thought it was? Are you starting to see how a dimwitted jackass is as capable of causing a monumental catastrophe as is a highly intelligent sociopath? Wise citizens know their limitations and will usually defer to our professional judgment. But our critics just can't seem to do that. They start at the end of an incident, and then reverse engineer it in their imagination, ignoring inconvenient facts along the way, in an effort to find some non-existent malevolent intent or incompetence on our part, or to come up with some other way that we could have achieved an outcome that is more emotionally satisfying to them. I do not believe they do this with pure motives. Their personal hostility towards cops is so intense that they apply their own psychologically warped spin to these events in the hope that they can convincingly paint us as monsters who are trying to satisfy some sadistic thirst for power at the expense of innocent people. They have a right to believe that if they want to. But they don't have the right to demand that the courts operate on that warped presupposition.

I KNOW MY RIGHTS

I don't know how many times I heard those words angrily fly from the lips of someone who was wearing my handcuffs, and who eventually ended up in a county jail or a state prison. This section might help you understand how your legal rights, which we do respect, fit into your legal responsibilities in relationship to your interaction with cops. That understanding will greatly reduce the possibility of you having an unpleasant or potentially injurious confrontation with them.

When people say, "I know my rights!," they are usually referring to some personally subjective concept that they have concocted in their own warped imaginations. Those rights have little to do with the first ten amendments to the constitution, also known as "The Bill of Rights." Most of the people who make the claim have either never read the amendments or didn't understand them. I'm not going to cover all of them here. Just the ones that cause cops the most exasperation when dealing with argumentative people. I'm not a lawyer, so my comments should not be interpreted as legal advice. But having done the job, read the case law, and taught in the police academy, I have a fair understanding of what your rights are within the context of the amendments when dealing with the police. It's just not that complicated. And I never gave anyone the legal justification to file a civil rights law suit against me for violating their rights. I don't doubt that some of the people I arrested consulted attorneys with that in mind. I'm equally confident that any attorneys who reviewed those cases would have told their client that there was no legal grounds for a civil rights case against me. So that should give you some confidence that I'm not leading you astray.

> **Amendment I:** "Congress shall make no law respecting an establishment of religion, or prohibiting the free exercise thereof; or abridging the freedom of speech, or of the press; or the right of the people peaceably to assemble, and to petition the government for a redress of grievances."

This amendment implicitly tells people what they can do by explicitly telling congress what it cannot do. That throws a monkey wrench into the plans of progressive politicians and social justice warriors who want their personal philosophy too be the law of the land. The right to practice your religious beliefs allows you to worship anything, or nothing at all. It gives you the right to assemble with people who share your faith and to corporately practice those beliefs. It gives you the right to publicly express those beliefs. It does not give you the right to sacrifice virgins (in the highly unlikely event that you could even find one in modern America), or to smoke crystal meth by claiming either of those practices as religious sacraments. You have a right to assemble and to petition the government for a redress of grievances. But the operative word in the amendment is "peaceably." You do not have the right to burn, loot, murder or injure other people, or damage their property. You do not have a right to block public roadways, sidewalks, and buildings, or to otherwise interfere with the lawful activity of other people. While a few bastions of liberal insanity tolerate mobs destroying public and private property, and terrorizing law abiding citizens, some states are not quite so forgiving. In Florida, for example, we have laws that ensure the rights of law abiding persons to defend themselves and their property. Here are a few Florida statutes and an explanation of how that works for the law abiding citizen. If you live outside of Florida, check your state's statutes. I suspect they have similar laws:

> **FSS 776.08** "Forcible felony" means treason; murder; manslaughter; sexual battery; carjacking; home-invasion robbery; robbery; burglary; arson; kidnapping; aggravated assault; aggravated battery; aggravated stalking; aircraft

piracy; unlawful throwing, placing, or discharging of a destructive device or bomb; and any other felony which involves the use or threat of physical force or violence against any individual."

FSS 776.012(2) - A person is justified in using or threatening to use deadly force if he or she reasonably believes that using or threatening to use such force is necessary to prevent imminent death or great bodily harm to himself or herself or another or to prevent the imminent commission of a forcible felony. A person who uses or threatens to use deadly force in accordance with this subsection does not have a duty to retreat and has the right to stand his or her ground if the person using or threatening to use the deadly force is not engaged in a criminal activity and is in a place where he or she has a right to be.

That last sentence in 776.012(2) is what is what is referred to as the "Stand your ground law." It isn't as much a new law as it is a clarification of an already existing statute. It means that, if you are in a place where you have a legal right to be, and you are not engaged in criminal activity, and someone unlawfully threatens or attempts to commit a crime against you, you do not have to retreat or try to get away from them. You have the right to stand your ground and to meet force with force. If the crime they are committing is a forcible felony you can use deadly force if that force is reasonable under all of the circumstance. For example: If you are walking down a public sidewalk and you are confronted by a man waving a machete and demanding your wallet, you don't have to try to run away or interview him about his intent. You can pull your concealed firearm from under your shirt and shoot the man between the eyes. The man was committing a forcible felony against you and you can reasonably claim that you were in fear of death or great bodily harm. Sure, the police will conduct a thorough investigation and send their findings to the state attorney for review. But the police and the state attorney will probably find that you acted reasonably within your legal rights under the use of force statute. Modern progressives go crazy over that. They don't want law abiding people to be able to protect themselves. Unfortunately for those of you in states like California, New York, and a few others that are controlled by mentally ill or morally depraved politicians, those same actions will probably land you in prison. Don't blame us. You elected them.

> **Amendment II**: A well-regulated Militia, being necessary to the security of a free State, the right of the people to keep and bear Arms, shall not be infringed.

Contrary to what anti-gun proponents want you to believe, most cops are not on their side. Cops prefer criminal control rather than gun control. Sure, there are a few brainwashed young rookies who drank the Kool-Aid served by their liberal teacher. And there are a few spineless law enforcement administrators who sold their souls to the devil for an invite to the White House and a photo op with a president, or to be considered for a federal job appointment. But those folks are a small minority. It only appears that there are more of them than there actually are because the propagandists in the mainstream media give them as much publicity as possible.

Why second amendment opponents have so much difficulty understanding the simple words, ". . .the right of the people to keep and bear arms, shall not be infringed." is a mystery. Of the fourteen words in that clause, twelve of them are single syllable English words. The other two words only have two syllables each. All of the words are common English with simple unambiguous definitions. And they are arranged in an easily understandable clause. In the 2008 case, District of Columbia vs Heller, the US Supreme Court held that the "Second Amendment protects an individual right to possess a firearm unconnected with service in a militia, and to use that arm for traditionally lawful purposes, such as self-defense within the home." That right extends to places beyond the home when necessary to protect one's self from serious bodily injury or death at the hands of violent criminals. Good cops who swore an oath to protect and defend the constitution took that oath seriously. They have no desire to disarm law abiding citizens or to aid federal law enforcement agencies from doing so. Most cops are sportsmen, hunters, competitive shooters, or military veterans who have families. More than a few of them are NRA members. They know that they will someday have to retire to civilian life, and that they will then be expected to abide by the same restrictions or disarmament that radical progressives want everyone else to abide by. They also know how dangerous society has become. Anyone with even a rudimentary understanding of history knows that the first thing a tyrannical despotic government does to enslave the civilian population is disarm them. Good cops don't want you to be disarmed any more than they want to be disarmed.

What is really behind the constant attempts by liberal politicians to disarm the law abiding populace? The answer is simple, and it has nothing to do with protecting you or your children from mass shootings or other gun related crimes. The goal is to render you, the law abiding citizen, powerless to successfully resist the tyranny of power-hungry political and social elitists whose delusional imaginary apotheosis convinces them that they have a divine right to force you to worship at their alter and bow to their will. Of course, if they achieve their goal, they will exempt themselves from the conditions they demand that you live by. They will surround themselves with heavily armed personal bodyguards. At that point, a lot of you are going to have to die in some very violent and bloody battles to recover the rights that you so carelessly surrendered.

The elitists will try to convince you that gun control and disarmament is necessary for you to accept as the only way to stop gun violence. They'll try to exploit the raw emotional reaction that you naturally have to reports of children and old people being killed in mass shootings at schools and shopping malls. Here are two wise quotes that address the elitists' "necessity" argument. One is from a speech that British Prime Minister William Pitt made before the House of Commons in November, 1783. The other is from Benjamin Franklin. You would do well to remember both of them every time any government official implicitly or explicitly tells you that infringing upon your second amendment right is necessary for the public safety:

> "Necessity is the plea for every infringement of human freedom: it is the argument of tyrants; it is the creed of slaves."
>
> - William Pitt

> "Those who would give up essential Liberty, to purchase a little temporary Safety, deserve neither Liberty nor Safety."
>
> - Benjamin Franklin

Look at the conditions in the countries around the world whose civilian populations voluntarily surrendered their guns to their governments or have been disarmed by military forces under the command of elitist politicians. The politicians in many of those countries have allowed hordes of immigrants with totally different cultural values to overrun those countries and terrorize the native civilian populations which are now at the mercy of those immigrants. The immigrants might not have guns either. But they do have knives, clubs, and numbers. And they have one other thing that gives them a distinct advantage over the native populations of the countries that they immigrate to; that advantage is cultures that are steeped in a violence and brutality that the native populations find impossible to grasp. Those immigrants have no intention of adopting the social and cultural values of the countries whose ruling politicians so foolishly allowed them in. If you're an American, do you really want to trust your elected officials with that kind of power and control over your life?

The politicians and elitists who want to delete the second amendment are the same clowns who promote criminal justice reforms that allow people to repeatedly commit crimes without going to jail or without posting bond. They're the same clowns who are in favor of lighter sentences or probation for repeat offenders. They're the same clowns who are in favor of criminals being released after serving only a fraction of their sentences. And they are the same clowns who call violent destructive criminals, "peaceful protesters." Whatever his shortcomings might have been, and in spite of the historical and social context of his remark, French clergyman and statesman Armand Jean du Plessis, Duke of Richelieu, 1585 – 1642, aka Cardinal Richelieu, got the concept right when he wrote:

> "Harshness towards individuals who flout the laws and commands of the state is for the public good; no greater crime against the public interest is possible than to show leniency to those who violate it."

But liberal elitist and their favorite politicians don't live in your world. They will never have to call 911 for police services as a result of their policies. You will. If the elitists have their way, you'll just have to rely on the goodwill of criminals, which is an oxymoron. Good luck with that. You see, the elitists value your life much less than they value their own philosophical dogmas. You are just a lab rat, and the world is their social experimentation laboratory. If their theories about gun control, criminal justice reforms, and nearly every other social issue is wrong, which they have repeatedly been proven to be, sacrificing your lives and the lives of those you love in order to test the theory just one more time is worth it to them. They will never admit that they are wrong. Disarming you is the key to enslaving you. It starts with small restrictions that you won't like, but will accept because you will think, "That's not so bad. I can live with that." Restrictions like limits on magazine capacity, bans on certain styles of rifles, ammo purchase limits, etc. Don't kid yourself. The objective of these elitist politicians today is the same as it was for their ideological predecessors in 1775 at Lexington and Concord. About seven hundred British Army regulars went there to capture and destroy military supplies reportedly stored by the Massachusetts militia. The objective was to render the civilian population incapable of defending themselves against the heavily armed troops of a tyrannical King and Parliament three thousand miles away. The only notable differences today is that King George's heavily armed troops have been replaced by agents of a rogue politicized US Department of Justice that operates like the Nazi Gestapo. King George and his parliament have been replaced by presidents and congress members who have more in common with Caligula than with any of America's founding fathers. These globalists are hellbent on becoming feudal lords and turning you into serfs who must grovel at their feet for food, shelter, and protection. They have to disarm you to accomplish that. And once you are disarmed, your only choices are submit or die. I'm amazed by how many Americans seem so willing to give up without a fight. For those who think my views are a bit extreme, consider these comments by some of America's founding fathers:

"An armed man is a citizen. An unarmed man is a subject."
- Thomas Jefferson

"The strongest reason for people to retain the right to keep and bear arms is, as a last resort, to protect themselves against tyranny in government."
- Thomas Jefferson

"No free man shall ever be debarred the use of arms."
- Thomas Jefferson

"Firearms are second only to the Constitution in importance; they are the peoples' liberty's teeth."
- George Washington

"A free people ought not only to be armed and disciplined, but they should have sufficient arms and ammunition to maintain a status of independence from any who might attempt to abuse them, which would include their own government."
- George Washington

"Arms in the hands of citizens may be used at individual discretion in private self-defense."
- John Adams

"To disarm the people is the most effectual way to enslave them."
- George Mason

"I ask sir, what is the militia? It is the whole people except for a few politicians."
- George Mason

"To preserve liberty, it is essential that the whole body of the people always possess arms, and be taught alike, especially when young, how to use them."
- Richard Henry Lee

"The Constitution shall never be construed to prevent the people of the United States who are peaceable citizens from keeping their own arms."
- Samuel Adams

"Guard with jealous attention the public liberty. Suspect everyone who approaches that jewel. Unfortunately, nothing will preserve it but downright force. Whenever you give up that force, you are ruined."

- Patrick Henry

"The right of self-defense is the first law of nature: in most governments it has been the study of rulers to confine this right within the narrowest limits possible. Wherever standing armies are kept up, and the right of the people to keep and bear arms is, under any color or pretext whatsoever, prohibited, liberty, if not already annihilated, is on the brink of destruction."

- St. George Tucker

"The right of the citizens to keep and bear arms has justly been considered as the palladium of the liberties of a republic; since it offers a strong moral check against the usurpation and arbitrary power of rulers; and will generally, even if these are successful in the first instance, enable the people to resist and triumph over them."

- Joseph Story

"What, Sir, is the use of a militia? It is to prevent the establishment of a standing army, the bane of liberty. . . . . Whenever Governments mean to invade the rights and liberties of the people, they always attempt to destroy the militia, in order to raise an army upon their ruins."

- Rep. Elbridge Gerry of Massachusetts

Amendment IV: "The right of the people to be secure in their persons, houses, papers, and effects, against unreasonable searches and seizures, shall not be violated, and no Warrants shall issue, but upon probable cause, supported by Oath or affirmation, and particularly describing the place to be searched, and the persons or things to be seized."

If a municipal, county, or state officer carelessly or maliciously violates that right, and subsequently charges someone with a crime as a result, the state attorney will probably discover it and will drop the charges before it goes anywhere. If not, a judge will throw the case out. Furthermore, the person whose right was violated can get redress and compensation through the courts. The officer might even be criminally charged. The hurdles that officers have to clear to obtain a search warrant are stringent. Judges do not rubber stamp warrant applications if the presenting officer has not cleared those hurdles. Finding a rare instance where a judge or officer made an error in the process does not mean that the process doesn't work. Having said that, the IV amendment right also has limits. Those limits are again found in that magic word, "Unreasonable." There are a few circumstances where warrantless searches are considered reasonable. I am not going to cover those exceptions here. But if such a warrantless search is contested, the determination of reasonableness will be decided by an impartial magistrate; not by the officer or by the person claiming the injury. With regard to a personal seizure (aka arrest), the IV amendment does not bestow the right to resist arrest. If a person being arrested does resist, officers have a right to use reasonable force to overcome that resistance. If the arrest or the amount of force used to effect the arrest is later determined by a judge or jury to be unlawful or unreasonable, the injured party can again seek redress through the courts and probably walk away with a substantial settlement. But the overwhelming majority of people who are injured or killed by police officers during an arrest suffer that fate as a direct result of their own unlawful resistance; not as a result of a constitutional violation on the part of the officer. In spite of that, critics try to blame the officer.

Fortunately for cops, the US Supreme Court decision in Graham vs Connor settled the use of force issue: "…all claims that law enforcement officers have used excessive force – deadly or not – in the course of an arrest, investigatory stop, or other seizure of a free citizen should be analyzed under the Fourth Amendment and its objective reasonableness standard…"

Whether or not a seizure or use of force was objectively reasonable is not something that the arrested person or their surviving family members get to emotionally and unilaterally decide. In Graham vs Conner, the court also said:

"The reasonableness of a particular use of force must be judged from the perspective of a reasonable officer on the scene, rather than with the 20/20 vision of hindsight."

In other words, courts consider whether or not the officer's actions were objectively reasonable under the totality of the facts and circumstances that the officer knew, should have known, or was dealing with at the time force was used. They also give the officer's training and experience appropriate consideration in evaluating how much force is reasonable. Likewise, if a person claims to be the victim of excessive force while being taken into custody for committing a crime, and was resisting arrest when the force was used, that will also be taken into consideration.

Cops hate having to use force or fight with people to take them into custody. It's extremely dangerous. Cops know that they can be seriously injured or killed when fighting with people. They can contract life threatening diseases from exposure to the blood or body fluids released by a suspect during a fight. They know that the suspects they have to fight with have lifestyles that make those suspects many times more likely to be infected with one or more of those diseases than are law abiding people. Their uniform and personal equipment can be damaged. If the person they have to fight is injured, that person is probably going to file a complaint, not because they have a legitimate reason, but because the threat of a law suit can sometimes be used as a bargaining chip to induce an agency to withdraw the charges in exchange for the plaintiff withdrawing the complaint. Here is another reason that cops hate fighting with people; a reason that critics and non-critics too quickly overlook. Cops carry guns and other weapons on their duty belt. If a cop gets into a fight with someone who was unarmed before the fight began, that person becomes instantly armed, technically if not legally, with everything on the officers belt the moment that the two of them become physically engaged. The number of officers who have been killed with their own guns after having suspects take their guns from them during fights is extremely troubling. I personally had several fights during my career when suspects tried to take my pistol. If the holsters my pistols were in were not retention holsters designed to make it difficult for anyone other than the person wearing it to remove the pistol, I would probably be dead.

Whether on foot or in a vehicle, a person is legally obligated to stop when ordered to do so by an officer. A person's subjective belief that they have done nothing wrong, or that the officer has no right to stop them, does not give that person a constitutional right to arbitrarily disregard the officer's order. Officers regularly stop people who believe they did nothing wrong. Malfunctioning brake lights are a good example. How do you know if your brake lights aren't working if no one tells you? Officers who stop people for malfunctioning brake lights will frequently let those people go with a verbal or written warning if the people were not aware of the defect. For minor infractions, most officers only detain the offender long enough to verify a valid driver's license and insurance coverage before releasing the offender with a citation or a warning. It doesn't take a genius to figure out that, if your brake lights aren't working and you have to stop suddenly, the vehicle behind you will probably slam into the back of your car, possibly injuring or killing you. And your malfunctioning brake lights will be recorded as a contributory factor in the cause of the crash. Would you rather an officer momentarily inconvenience you by stopping you to make you aware of the defect? Or would you rather be shredded by a heavily loaded eighteen-wheeler because the driver saw no brake lights and was unable to stop before running over you and your car? If you happen to be carrying a couple of kilos of cocaine or methamphetamine, I suppose you'll pick option two.

Perhaps you're walking down the street when an officer orders you to stop. He asks you if you have any weapons on you and then pats you down to be sure that you don't. You're incensed by this belligerent seizure because you've done nothing wrong. A minute later a police car arrives and stops about fifty feet away from you. Two people in the back seat look you over for about ten seconds. The officer who stopped you has a brief private radio conversation with the officer in the car before the car drives away. By now you're furious. But the officer knew something you didn't know. A convenience store was robbed two blocks from that location two minutes before the officer stopped you. The victim and witness who called 911 to report the crime described the suspect as a man whose clothing and physical description were very similar to yours. That description was broadcast to the officer who stopped you. The people in the police car were the victim and the witness. After looking you over, they told the officer that you were not the robber. The officer explains all of this to you. He apologizes for the inconvenience and he thanks you for your cooperation. How difficult was that? You assumed he was harassing you for no good reason when he was actually doing his job. Had you actually been the robber, and had the officer not stopped you because he was afraid that you might be annoyed and file a complaint against him, you would be free carry out your plan to rob another store a few blocks away. The clerk in that store would resist and you would shoot him. Do you think the dead clerk's family would be pleased that the police were more concerned about annoying you than they were about preventing you from killing their loved one?

Resisting or interfering with an officer in the lawful performance of his duty is not a constitutional right. Your complaint that the officer's actions were not legally justified will not be evaluated based on your petulant subjective annoyance. It will be evaluated based on whether or not the officer's actions were objectively reasonable in light of the totality of the circumstances and the information the officer had at the time of the event. It would be enormously helpful if people would give officers the benefit of the doubt, and at least a little bit of credit for personal and professional integrity, instead of jumping to the conclusion that officers are sadistically harassing them for no good reason.

Does that mean you have no recourse if an officer does something that you think is unprofessional or illegal? It does not. But perhaps you should make a polite inquiry with his supervisor or command staff before jumping to a conclusion and filing a complaint. There might be circumstances that you were not aware of that will cause you to see the event in a different light. If you still are not satisfied, you can file a formal complaint. Contrary to the false narrative promoted by the critics, police agencies that white-wash complaints are extremely few and far between. The odds are overwhelmingly in favor of your complaint being thoroughly and impartially investigated. Police administrators do not want rogue officers on their departments. Those officers are a serious threat, not only to the public, but to the agency as a whole and to good officers individually. Does that mean your complaint will be resolved to your satisfaction? No. There is a long history of people filing false or frivolous complaints against police officers. Those complaints have declined since the advent of dash cameras in cop cars and body cameras being worn by officers. The reason for the decline should be self-evident. If your allegation of illegal or unprofessional conduct by an officer cannot be adequately substantiated, it would not be fair to charge or discipline that officer based on your word alone. If the agency's investigation concludes that the officer committed a criminal offense, they will file criminal charges against the officer. As previously explained, the state attorney might not prosecute if he does not think the case can be proven beyond a reasonable doubt. The agency will still fire the officer. But keep in mind that officers have rights. If your complaint is that an officer's behavior was unprofessional rather than criminal, that is not necessarily grounds for the officer to be terminated or disciplined. Consider these two hypothetical scenarios that might cause you to file a complaint about the officer's behavior:

1. *An officer stops you for speeding. You are respectful and cooperative. He writes a citation. As he hands it to you, he angrily says, "Slow down, asshole!"*

2. *An officer stops you for speeding. He is professional and polite. He writes a citation and hands it to you. You snatch the citation from his hand as you angrily say, "You're an asshole! I hope somebody shoots you today!" The officer smiles and calmly replies, "Have a nice day, dick head!" as he returns to his cruiser.*

In either case, while arguably unprofessional, neither officer did anything worthy of termination. They probably breached a department policy related to officer conduct for which they might be disciplined. In the first case, if the agency reviews the body camera footage and substantiates the accuracy of your complaint, the officer probably won't be fired, especially if he has a reasonably clean employment record. He might be sent for a psychological evaluation to determine if he is still fit for duty. Or he might be required to attend anger management training as a condition for continued employment. It might be that his conduct was an anomaly due to him being under some unusual stress. Maybe he just found out that his wife was having an adulterous affair with their next door neighbor while he was working midnight shift. Maybe he discovered that the child he has emotionally bonded with and has been raising for the past fifteen years is actually the offspring of that neighbor. Firing an experienced and talented officer for a momentary lapse of judgment brought on by unusually stressful circumstances makes no sense if the officer can be salvaged by some time off, remedial training, counseling, and the moral support of his coworkers and supervisors.

In the second case, if the agency reviews the body camera footage and sees your behavior, the officer is more likely to receive a chuckling verbal reprimand and pat on the back from the chief, along with a reminder to not let idiots like you bait him into exchanging insults.

In any event, if an officer does something that you honestly believe is wrong, and you do not make a reasonable inquiry or file a complaint if appropriate, don't talk trash about the officer and the agency. You owe the agency an opportunity to investigate. Depending on whether or not your complaint is valid, that investigation has several possible beneficial outcomes for the agency.

1. *If the complaint is valid, it will let them get rid of a bad officer, or at least put the officer on their radar as a previously undiscovered potential problem child; or*

2. *If the complaint is not valid, it will let them put you on the radar as a paranoid whackadoodle that they will probably have to deal with in the future.*

Another area where some people think their IV amendment rights are violated is when they are stopped for some minor infraction. If the officer happens to be white, and the person stopped is clearly from a different racial or ethnic group, the person stopped will sometimes assume that the officer was racially or ethnically profiling. Unfounded racial and ethnic profiling accusations have become a chronic annoyance for law enforcement agency leaders. Cops do profile. But that profiling is not based on color or ethnicity. It is based on conduct and circumstances. If an officer sees a man holding a bag at the back door of a closed business at 2am, he doesn't care what color or ethnicity the man is. He is going to check the man out to see what he is up to. Law abiding people usually are not holding a bag at the back door of closed businesses at 2am. If that man happens to be of an obvious racial or ethnic minority, and he has identification and credentials as a janitorial maintenance contractor hired to clean the business after hours, and the bag contains trash that he was taking to the dumpster, the encounter will be brief. The officer will wish the contractor a good evening and the contractor can continue with his janitorial duties. If the officer isn't busy, he might even stick around for a few minutes to make sure that no nighttime predators come along and bother the contractor. If the man happens to be white, has no identification, no reasonable explanation for his presence, and the bag contains gloves and a screw driver, the man will be on his way to jail for loitering and prowling. That's profiling.

When people are committing, or are about to commit a crime, they often display behavioral cues. Race and ethnicity are not behavioral cues. The more highly trained and experienced an officer is, the more adept he is at recognizing small behavioral cues that are completely unrelated to race or ethnicity. Since untrained inexperienced people don't notice these cues, their default assumption is that there were no cues and that the officer is profiling based on race or ethnicity. If a person does not exhibit any cues that give an officer reasonable suspicion for an investigatory stop, the officer still has a right to watch that person. If the person is up to no good, it probably won't take long before they commit some minor offense that does give the officer legal justification for an investigatory stop. The fact that the officer might not normally stop people for such minor offenses does not mean that he has to ignore everyone who commits them. In Wren v US, 1996, the Supreme Court ruled unanimously that pretext stops are lawful as long as a legitimate violation occurred. The officer's ulterior motive doesn't matter. The moral of the story is, obey the law and you probably won't get stopped. I say probably because there are circumstance where an officer might stop you when you have done nothing wrong. For example, the vehicle you are driving matches the description of one that was recently reported as stolen or used in a crime. Or you match the physical description of someone who was reported as a missing or endangered person. Or a loved one contacted the police because of a family emergency and requested that the police notify you of the emergency. That is not profiling. The officer is conducting the stop based upon information provided by other credible or known sources. The details of where that information came from is probably recorded in a report, or in the CAD (computer aided dispatch system), or in a 911 audio recording. If an officer stops you under those circumstances, he will detain you only long enough to verify that the vehicle is not the one reported stolen, or that you are not the missing / endangered person, or the family member being sought. However, if there is a bong with white residue in the bowl sticking out of the ash tray, or there is acrid smoke that smells like chemicals or cleaning products lingering in your car, the fact that the officer's initial contact with you was for some non-criminal reason does not mean that he has to ignore indicators that you were recently smoking methamphetamine. He's going to investigate and your complaint of profiling will evaporate. Obey the law and behave like a responsible adult and any contact that you have with an officer will likely be brief and polite.

> **Amendment V:** No person shall be held to answer for a capital, or otherwise infamous crime, unless on a presentment or indictment of a Grand Jury, except in cases arising in the land or naval forces, or in the Militia, when in actual service in time of War or public danger; nor shall any person be subject for the same offense to be twice put in jeopardy of life or limb; nor shall be compelled in any criminal case to be a witness against himself, nor be deprived of life, liberty, or property, without due process of law; nor shall private property be taken for public use, without just compensation.

Most of that amendment has more to do with courts and attorneys than with cops. If someone is arrested for "a capital, or otherwise infamous crime," even if police have tons of evidence that the person is guilty, the prosecutor will still take the evidence before a grand jury to obtain an indictment before trying to take the person to trial. At least that is what they are supposed to do. There are instances where prosecutors circumvent the grand jury process for political reasons. One such case was the previously mentioned case where the officer shot the fleeing motorcyclist. Why would an experienced state attorney go out of her way to avoid presenting her case to a grand jury? Because she knew that her case was so weakened by the equivocal nature of the evidence that a grand jury would be unlikely to give her the indictment that she wanted. So she filed the case directly and took the officer to trial on manslaughter charges. And, as already mentioned, the officer was finally acquitted. Another case where the grand jury was circumvented was the previously mentioned case of the State of Florida vs George Zimmerman. Based on the crime scene evidence, Zimmerman's statements and physical injuries, the state attorney in the judicial circuit where the event occurred determined that there was insufficient evidence to charge Zimmerman or to take the case before a grand jury because the evidence supported Zimmerman's actions falling within the parameters of the use of force statute. But a few very noisy agitators wanted to racially exploit the incident. The Governor caved in to the pressure and assigned the case to a special prosecutor from a different judicial circuit. In short, a post-menopausal harpy was handed a political hatchet to try to hack Zimmerman to pieces to satisfy the blood lust of angry agitators. She reopened the case and brought in her own investigators. Those investigators threw their professional integrity into the toilet and gave her the probable cause affidavit that she wanted to charge Zimmerman. Did she present the case to a grand jury? No. Second degree murder might be considered infamous, but it isn't a capital crime. That gave her the wiggle room she needed to circumvent the grand jury and file the case directly. Why would she do that? For the same reason the state attorney in the other case did it. She knew that a grand jury would never give her an indictment. So she took the case to trial without an indictment and cost tax payers close to a million dollars to prosecute a losing case. Zimmerman was found not guilty.

My purpose in recounting those two cases as related to the amendment in question is to point out that it was not law enforcement that trampled the rights of the officer and George Zimmerman. It was politically power hungry prosecutors. Had those events been left to grand juries in the judicial circuit where they occurred, as they should have been, there would have been no indictments, no trials, and millions of dollars of tax payer money would not have been wasted on a losing cases.

Another part of the fifth amendment that often confuses people is the part that says no person, " . . shall be compelled in any criminal case to be a witness against himself. . ." That is the portion of the amendment that the Miranda warning is based upon. (See Miranda vs Arizona, 384 U.S. 436) Almost everyone has heard the Miranda warning given by television and movie cops; at least enough of it to be confused. A typical Miranda warning would go something like this.

- You have the right to remain silent.
- Anything you say can be used against you in court.
- You have the right to talk to a lawyer before we ask you any questions.
- You have the right to have a lawyer with you during questioning.
- If you cannot afford a lawyer, one will be appointed for you before any questioning if you wish.
- If you decide to answer questions now without a lawyer present, you have the right to stop answering at any time.

Some people who are arrested claim that their rights were violated because the officer did not read them their rights at the time of the arrest. A Miranda warning is not automatically required when someone is arrested. It applies to custodial interrogation. That means being questioned while in custody; or being questioned under circumstances that would give a person a reasonable belief that they were not free to leave. Under those circumstance officers are obliged to advise the person of their Miranda rights before questioning. If officers fail to Mirandize the person before questioning, any incriminating statements the person makes will likely be declared inadmissible in court. Furthermore, evidence recovered as a result of those statements will likely be excluded also. But officers don't have to Mirandize people just because the person is arrested. I sometimes arrested people because they had outstanding arrest warrants. Or sometimes I had all of the probable cause I needed to arrest them and I didn't need to ask them any questions. In fact, there were many times that I didn't even talk to them after arresting them. If I didn't talk to them after arresting them, they couldn't accuse me of questioning them. Since people love to talk, statements that they made that were not in response to me questioning them or talking to them were not protected under Miranda and were admissible in court. In each case where a defense attorney motioned to have their clients statements excluded because I did not Mirandize their client, the judge denied the motion and allowed the statement to be admitted when it became clear that I did not question or even speak to them. There are also cases where an officer might question someone during what would be considered a consensual encounter. If an officer walks up to a known drug dealer on a public sidewalk and says, "Hey man. Are you holding any drugs?" the drug deal doesn't have to talk to the officer. He can walk away or simply ignore the officer. If he says, "Yeah. You got me." and then reaches into his pocket and pulls out a bag of crystal meth and hands it to the officer, the dealer cannot make a legitimate claim that he wasn't Mirandized. The officer didn't command him to stop, and didn't do anything to give him the impression that he was not free to leave or that he had to answer questions. It was a consensual encounter. There is also an exemption to giving a Miranda warning when questioning is necessary for public safety. For example, the person has knowledge of the whereabouts of an explosive device that could jeopardize public safety.

> **Amendment VI:** In all criminal prosecutions, the accused shall enjoy the right to a speedy and public trial, by an impartial jury of the State and district wherein the crime shall have been committed, which district shall have been previously ascertained by law, and to be informed of the nature and cause of the accusation; to be confronted with the witnesses against him; to have compulsory process for obtaining witnesses in his favor, and to have the assistance of Counsel for his defense.

That's what people have attorneys for. Cops have no control over whether or not someone hires an attorney or gets a speedy trial. That's up to the lawyers involved. If a person doesn't get a speedy trial, it's probably because they waived the right. That's not our fault. It was their choice.

Almost everything that happens to a person after their arrest is determined by their attorney, the prosecuting attorney, and a judge. But cops are the guys who get blamed because they are the ones who arrested the defendant. A cop in a sharp uniform with a shiny badge and a gun makes a much more attractive target than a prosecuting attorney in an ill-fitting blue suit with clashing brown shoes. I'm not mocking the fashion sense of prosecutors. I'm just pointing out that uniforms make cops easy and attractive targets. Nobody calls a prosecuting attorney "Nazi!" for not being stylish.

> **Amendment VIII:** Excessive bail shall not be required, nor excessive fines imposed, nor cruel and unusual punishments inflicted.

Again, cops don't set bail, impose fines, or determine punishment. But eventually they get the blame for all of it because they are the ones who make the arrests.

DO THE STATS SUPPORT THE NARRATIVE?

Since I'm in Florida, I'll use Florida as an example to answer that question. In 2017 there were approximately 46,000 sworn law enforcement officers in Florida. In that same year there were roughly 711,000 arrests for all forms of crime. That averages out to roughly 1,900 arrests per day. With that number of officers and that number of arrests, if the narrative that police brutality was as systemic as critics say it is, it would be reasonable to expect that dozens of people of every race, ethnicity and gender would be shot to death or seriously injured by officers every day. But that isn't the case. Even in the face of violent physical resistance, most officers make an effort to take criminals into custody without injuring or killing them. But the news media doesn't report the number of arrested people who aren't injured or killed while resisting arrest. Have you ever heard a journalist ask a convicted criminal who had served his sentence if he was treated respectfully by the arresting officer who arrested him? Or, if he did get a few bumps or bruises during the arrest, if he might have done something that contributed to it? I've talked to a lot of criminals over the years. It might surprise you to know some of them turned their lives around. They are honest enough to admit that their arrest was justified, that the police treated them fairly, or that they deserved the few bumps and bruises that they did receive. Some of them admit that, if they had not been arrested and thumped a few times in the process, they would probably have continued their wicked ways and ended up dead or serving life in prison. On several occasions, people that I arrested approached me in public several years later. They apologized for their behavior and they thanked me for treating them with more gentleness and respect than their behavior entitled them to. How did I react? I accepted their apology. I thanked them for taking the time to apologize. I told them that I was happy to hear that they got their lives back on track and I wished them well. Who among us has not done something stupid that we regretted after taking some time to reflect on our behavior? Considering the number of people who resist arrest, and the level of that resistance, what is truly remarkable is the restraint exercised by officers, and the extremely small percentage of people who are injured or killed during those encounters.

Earlier I used a simple traffic infraction to illustrate a few points. If you consider the thousands of people who get cited or arrested each day in America, and how many of those people are verbally aggressive or physically resist arrest, you'll have a small idea of how hazardous, not to mention irritating, even something as simple as a minor traffic stop can become.

HOW THINGS HAVE CHANGED

Can you think of one profession or organization that does not have some management or labor problems, even if those problems are minor ones? Why should it come as a surprise to anyone that law enforcement has similar problems? Human beings are flawed creatures with a natural bent towards selfishness, greed, and dishonesty. Any organization that has to employ human beings in order to function is going to have a few problems and problem children. But most of the problems in law enforcement don't come from the practitioners' bent towards selfishness, greed, and dishonesty as much as they come from the delusional expectations of our critics. Officers who do things that are improper, or sometimes illegal, are usually branded by critics as "bad cops" with malicious dispositions and evil intentions. The reality is that they are more often just unqualified people who should not have been hired in the first place. How does that happen? A long time ago, officer pay and benefits were poor. The men (and yes, I said men) who wanted to be police officers had honorable motives that had less to do with money and benefits as with protecting their communities. The men who were hired usually did not have college degrees. What they did have was a natural aptitude for the work. They had a gift for spotting bad guys, and they had the boldness to tangle with the bad guys when necessary. All applicants had to meet the same minimum standards to be considered for the job. Those standards included civil service exams, physical exams, polygraph exams, background investigations, and oral interviews. There were also minimum height and weight requirements. It was understood that officers would occasionally have to physically fight with bad people. So agencies set minimum physical requirements to ensure that the men who were hired as officers would be intimidating enough to discourage most people from fighting; and if people did fight, the officer would be strong and skilled enough to have a good chance of surviving if not winning the fight. There were no federal court rulings that required agencies to make accommodations for applicants who did not meet those standards. As the latter half of the twentieth century progressed, officer pay and benefits improved. That improvement began to attract applicants who were motivated by selfish or less than honorable motives. And because of new federal court rulings, agencies had to start hiring people whose job applications would have been rejected a few years before. The egalitarian political and social forces that brought the law suits that resulted in those court rulings got what they wanted. Objective standards were tossed out the window and agencies are now required to consider additional factors that are unrelated to applicant aptitude and ability; factors such as gender, race, and ethnicity. Agencies can no longer require all applicants to meet the same minimal mental, physical, and moral standards. Doing so would negatively affect the agency's gender, racial and ethnic demographics and expose them to potential civil liabilities in court. Now, when officers have performance failures, critics don't blame the courts for idiotic decisions; they blame the chief administrators for a lack of leadership. But it is rarely the administrator's fault. Police administrators today sometimes have to hold their nose when swearing in new officers. Why? Because administrators have to fish for employees from a shallow and stagnant applicant pool that is contaminated with incompetent and unqualified people. Filling positions from that pool is a difficult proposition at best. How did those people get into that pool? Years ago, at least in Florida, and I suspect in many other states, people who attended police academies had to be sponsored by a law enforcement agency that had already done a preliminary screening of the person and had at least a tentative plan to hire them. Now many police academies are under the control of the state's Department of Education college and university system. Pay the tuition fee, and you can go to a police academy as long as you sign the hold harmless forms. City managers and mayors tell their law enforcement agencies' chief administrators that the departments' gender, racial and ethnic demographics must reflect community demographics, regardless of how that goal is achieved. The chiefs know that many of the people in the applicant pool are disasters waiting to happen. If a chief does hire them, all he can do is hope that the disasters are not serious enough to cause an innocent person to be harmed, or to cause the agency to be seriously embarrassed or sued before the chief can retire and collect his pension. Even more troubling is that chiefs not only have to consider an applicant's gender, race and ethnicity in the hiring process, but they also have to make sure that some of the persons hired from those groups are promoted to supervisory or leadership positions, regardless of the lack of competence or lack of leadership ability demonstrated by those persons. It's a numbers game. Since police agencies operate on tax dollars, liberal social and political power brokers demand that those agencies have employee ratios that reflect the diversity of the community in question. That places the general public in substantial danger. It doesn't matter if the promoted employees are blithering idiots or moral nightmares, as long as they fit the liberal's Utopian demographic dream. Chief administrators are not opposed to hiring qualified gender, racial or ethnic minorities. Such opposition would be counterproductive. Hiring the best candidate for the job, regardless of gender, race or ethnicity, is in the chief's best interest. The more competent the officers are, the more cohesive the agency is, and the safer the community is. And the safer the community is, the better the chief looks. But when a mayor or city manager orders an agency's chief administrator to only consider applicants from a particular gender, racial, or ethnic minority, regardless of any other factors, it puts that administrator in a very bad position. Many agencies have difficulty attracting applicants from those minorities. And when they do have those applicants, it is not unusual for the applicant's criminal history, civil service exam performance, physical or medical conditions, drug use, or psychological evaluation to disqualify them from further consideration. So, in order to satisfy the mayor or city manager, the chief must either lower or totally disregard the hiring standards that were originally established with public safety in mind.

In the mid nineteen eighties, I had a conversation with a woman who, after more than twenty-five years of service, was getting ready to retire as the human resource manager of a large law enforcement agency in Florida. She told me that she had grown to hate the job that she once loved. She said that she saw the job applications and the civil service exam results of every officer applicant for the previous twenty years. She told me that an increasing number of those applicants were functionally illiterate. She described hand written job applications that appeared to have been completed by third graders. Illegible hand writing. Simple common words spelled phonetically. Grammar and syntax errors that made applications nearly unintelligible. Sentences written in the jargon, slang, or broken English of the applicant; job applicants who could not speak, read, write, or understand common English well enough to follow the application and test instructions, or to accurately collect information from complainants, victims or witnesses well enough to write an intelligible accurate police report. Over her objections, some of those applicants were being hired over better qualified applicants in order to make the agency's demographic profile meet the demands of higher government officials. Failure to meet those demands could result in a chief administrator being fired. A man who has survived long enough to rise through the ranks and become a chief administrator isn't going to risk losing his job on a matter of principle when he has a mortgage to pay and a family to support. But this lady from human resources had become too frustrated to continue. She told me that her kids were grown and her house was almost paid off. She said that she was becoming physically ill from the stress of knowing that the public safety, which she felt responsible to protect by trying to ensure that the most qualified applicants were hired, was being jeopardized by police administrators who were being blackmailed into hiring unqualified applicants for the sake of appeasing bureaucrats and politicians. This situation, as described by this loyal public servant, is now systemic in municipal, county, state, and federal government; and not just in law enforcement. But the dangerous and complex nature of law enforcement makes hiring incompetent or unqualified officers much more potentially explosive than in any other type of government service. Here is a real example that demonstrates the problem. A small city had an opening for police chief and was interviewing applicants. Because members of the community complained that the police department had no black officers, the city council pointedly asked each candidate what he was going to do to hire more black officers. The candidate who got the job was not the best qualified. But he answered the question with what the city council want to hear; "Whatever it takes." Since there were no black applicants, and no black police cadets in the nearest police academies, the new chief kept his word and went to a police academy a hundred and thirty miles away to try to recruit officers from the half dozen or so black cadets in that class. Two of them applied. The agency that sponsored one of those cadets to the academy had planned on hiring him when he graduated. But when he failed a pre-employment polygraph, and then admitted that he lied during the polygraph, that agency withdrew its employment offer. In spite of that, the new chief offered him a job. The investigator who conducted his background investigation found a number of very troubling issues in the applicant's past. The investigator viewed that applicant as a serious potential liability and recommended that he not be hired. The chief ignored the investigator's warning and hired him anyway. That applicant didn't make it out of the field training program before being terminated because his field training officers caught him lying on several occasions. It also didn't help that off duty officers and several other credible citizens reported seeing him driving recklessly around town in his personal sports car. The other applicant was also hired in spite of a checkered past. He barely made it through the field training program. After he went solo, he made some foolish mistakes that a probationary rookie would normally have been fired for. But the chief kept him anyway. That officer quit about a year later to join the military. The agency was right back where it started before the new chief was hired. Then a black applicant showed up who looked promising. He was a twenty-five year veteran officer who had recently retired as a detective sergeant from a large metropolitan agency about a hundred and fifty miles away. He had recently moved to the area and wanted to continue his police career in a smaller and less stressful environment. Based on his experience and his position at his previous agency, it was a forgone conclusion that he would breeze through the hiring process. When he wasn't hired, I asked the agency's deputy chief what happened. He told me that the gentleman failed the reading comprehension section of the civil service exam and could no longer be considered. Ironically, this man had been a supervisor in a criminal investigation unit of the agency that he retired from. In another case, a chief administrator wanted to fill an opening in his detective bureau. Two officers applied. Both were white, in their mid-twenties, and had a little over a year of experience. One of them was a well-disciplined and psychologically stable, married man. He was a fit, six foot, hundred and ninety pound army veteran with a high school diploma and combat experience. The other was a five and a half foot, hundred and fifteen pound lesbian with a two year degree in criminal justice and an argumentative attitude. The lesbian got the job. The clearly better qualified male officer was angry about not getting the position. He stayed with the agency, but began looking for employment elsewhere. The female quit without notice about a year later because she and her "significant other" decided to move to the South Pacific and get married.

Police administrators want officers who are honest, have good moral character, are psychologically stable, have good critical thinking skills, can make rational decisions under extreme stress, and can hold their own in a physical fight if necessary. How many people can you think of today between 20 and 40 years-old who possess those qualities? A 50 year-old veteran officer who has survived twenty five years on the street doesn't care about the gender, race, or ethnicity of his coworkers. What he cares about is whether or not those coworkers, who sooner or later are going to have to back him up on a hot call, have the intelligence and verbal skills to deescalate a tense situation when possible; the physical ability and intestinal fortitude to fight or kill if deescalation isn't possible; and the good judgment to know the difference between the two. That immediately eliminates all of the female applicants and a sizable percentage of the males. That's not sexist. It's a physical and psychological fact of life in twenty-first century America. Men and women are physically and psychologically different. Those differences are not nullified by the wishful thinking of feminists and liberal ideologues. An argument about whether or not those differences are the result of evolutionary biology or the design of a wise creator is irrelevant in the present context. As for the men, many of them were emasculated by their single mothers or by educational and cultural institutions run by emotional women who consider masculinity to be "toxic" and anathema.

Time and time again during my career, I personally witnessed the lives of male officers, including my own life, being jeopardized by female officers whose physical strength, coordination, technical skill, courage and judgment were frighteningly deficient for the task at hand. I'm not saying those female officers were not nice people, or that they did not try. Many of them were and did. But being a cop isn't a popularity contest. It is sometimes physically arduous, frequently psychologically stressful, and nearly always extremely unforgiving of shortcomings and mistakes.

I was an adjunct instructor at a regional public service academy for more than a decade. In addition to regular law enforcement and corrections subjects, I also taught what are called "high liability subjects." Those subjects included first aid, firearms, and defensive tactics. The natural physical and psychological differences between the male and female cadets was obvious. The male cadets were bigger, stronger, faster, harder to injure, and much harder to psychologically rattle than the female cadets. The few male cadets who were shorter and weighted less than some of the larger female cadets still had a notable genetic power to weight ratio advantage in terms of speed, strength, and psychological stability, and not by a small margin. During defensive tactics training, I and the other instructors had to go out of our way to ensure that the male cadets did not injure the female cadets during practice. It wasn't realistic to pair females with other females for practice. Our job was to prepare all of the cadets for the kind of real world encounters they were likely to have on the job. How do you do that without injuring the female cadets? You can't. During first aid, when it came time to perform emergency drags or carries, the natural body fat to muscle mass ratio difference between the female and male cadets was evident. The females had more difficulty than male cadets. During firearms training, unless they had extensive prior training and experience, the female cadets had more difficulty developing the skills needed to qualify. They often required additional one on one instruction. Their hands were smaller and their hand, arm, and upper body strength made it more difficult for them to consistently and repeatedly actuate the slide and reload the magazines on auto pistols. When shooting revolvers, many of them experienced muscle fatigue that hindered their ability to repeatedly press the trigger, reload, and get consistent shot groups. Those differences became critical when training them on the twelve-gauge shotgun. Shorter arms and less upper body strength, coupled with the ergonomics and heavy recoil of the shotgun, made that weapon intimidating and nearly unmanageable for most of the female cadets. We knew that, if they ever got hired, most of them would never take their shotgun from its rack, even if their life or the life of another officer depended on it. And if they did take it out of the rack and used it, it was highly unlikely that they would hit the person who needed to be neutralized. Missing a dangerous adversary with a load of buckshot or a slug can be an unhappy event for any living creature that is behind the adversary.

Instructors that I spoke with from other academies acknowledged the same problems with their female cadets. Any cadet who failed any high liability section would have to take and pass that section again in a future academy class. On the rare occasions that a male cadet would fail one of those sections, that cadet responded by being angry with himself and would make a commitment to practice hard in the interim so he would be ready when the next academy class came around. How did the female cadets handle their failure? Most of them cried. Yes, cried! These issues might be a tolerable annoyance in an instructional setting. But it can become a life or death issue during a real-life situation where proficiency and emotional stability are critical.

Critics who consider male officers misogynists for not wanting to work with female officers don't have skin in the game. I doubt that those critics would be so sanctimoniously egalitarian if a six-foot four-inch, two-hundred and eighty pound, escaped murderer was trying to kick their door in. Who do you think they would want to respond to their 911 call for help? A five and a half foot, hundred and fifteen pound female, or a six foot, hundred and ninety pound male combat veteran?

So, what happens when these female recruits are hired and their obvious deficiencies become a glaring liability? They get promoted to positions that get them off the road and out of harm's way. In a radically feminized progressive culture, these women have been brainwashed into believing that they deserve the promotions. When they end up in supervisory positions, they become unnecessarily authoritarian or confrontational towards their male subordinates. And, when some of them end up as chief administrators, and then screw up because they are incompetent, they blame their agency's deteriorating morale and declining performance statistics on a lack of cooperation by the rank and file male officers instead of their own incompetence and lack of leadership ability.

What do these issues have to do with our critics? Our critics are the same philosophical elitists who are driving the hiring practices and policies in every field of endeavor, including law enforcement. Who suffers from this? You, the law abiding citizens, male and female, that depend upon law enforcement officers for protection.

DEFUND THE POLICE

It's remarkable to see how many cop critics are onboard with defunding the police. Those critics are the first to call 911 when something goes bump in the night outside their home or office. I don't know who those critics think is going to protect them after they defund the police, but it won't be us. Most cops like their jobs. But they aren't going to do those jobs under the restrictions and conditions that the critics want to impose. And they aren't going to do those jobs for free. In the current cop-hating atmosphere, many officers are reactive rather than proactive, doing only enough work to keep their jobs until they can retire and collect their pensions. Most veteran cops have multiple job skills and can find other work. And, assuming the cop resigned or retired under honorable circumstances, most prospective employers see him as a potential asset because they know he was thoroughly vetted before being hired as a cop. In fact, the depth of investigation he went through to become a cop is legally prohibited for most private sector employers. And, if he successfully carried his officer responsibilities long enough to retire or resign under honorable circumstances, he is a much better risk than someone who was a barista by day and a Twitter blogger or Instagram influencer by night. For the officer, once he purges from his system the excess adrenaline that he had to maintain to survive, working in a less stressful job would be a pleasant change.

The other people who want to defund the police are socialists and anarchists who hate America and want to destroy it from within. It's amazing to see how many of those cretins are high ranking politicians or bureaucrats. These politicians and bureaucrats are so driven by their radical agenda and secular philosophies that they haven't noticed the angry law abiding citizens who are fed up with their shenanigans. Those law abiding citizens have been standing down only because of the thin buffer that cops have been barely able to maintain between them and the cultural terrorists that the politicians and bureaucrats have been unleashing on society. Take us out of the equation, and those citizens will become organized vigilantes who will start hunting down and killing the terrorists on sight. When the politicians and bureaucrats who defunded us start begging us to come back to deal with the vigilantes, we'll simply reply, "No thanks, cupcake! We're done! And besides, we have a vigilante meeting to go to this evening."

Some misguided souls think that defunding the police would mean a national federalized police force would be established. That is a very bad idea with impossible barriers. This is the United States. That means a republic composed of independent states that maintain a considerable level of sovereignty. Federal law enforcement officers can only enforce federal laws. They do not have the authority to enforce individual state laws unless granted that authority by those states individually. There are very few state chief executives who are stupid enough to surrender their power and their state's sovereignty to power hungry federal politicians and bureaucrats. Each state has its own unique blend of demographics, geography, climate, infrastructure, resources and challenges. A one size fits all approach to law enforcement won't work without totally destroying a state's sovereignty. And state sovereignty is about the only thing protecting states from the sheer insanity that infects the federal government.

Each state legislature passes laws that are consistent with the values of their citizens, within the reasonable framework of the federal constitution. Legislators and chief executives of conservative states are more inclined to interpret the constitution in the plain English in which it was written, and within the historical context and understanding of the men who wrote it. Legislators and chief executives in liberal states interpret the constitution according to their own convoluted philosophy and linguistic gymnastics in an attempt to use the constitution as a cudgel with which to beat their ideological opponents into submission. How does that work? Simple. Declare things illegal today that were legal yesterday, and people who were good law abiding citizens yesterday will automatically become felonious criminals. Then federal law enforcement officers can burn those citizens alive inside their residences, or shoot them in the face with a high powered rifle from two hundred yards away while they stand unarmed in the doorways of their homes, holding their infant children in their arms. In other words, try, convict, and execute them without a trial or any other due process.

You think defunding your police in favor of a federal police force sounds good? How good do you think it will sound when you call what used to be your police department and you reach a recording that says, "The number you have reached is no longer in service," or "Your call will be answered in the order it was received. You are caller number twenty-six. Your approximate wait time is one hour." How good do you think it will sound when your neighbor calls to complain about your dog barking at a cat at 11 P.M. and a federal swat team shows up, shoots your dog, kicks your door down and terrorizes your family while they conduct an illegal search of your home?

RACISM

Racism is an ugly human attribute, regardless of the race of the person displaying it or the race of the person who it is being displayed towards. Whether or not that racism is a private personal opinion or is overtly manifested by some act or omission are two different things and should be treated as such. The accusation that racism is systemic in law enforcement is a lie. An isolated racist act by a small fraction of individuals, regardless of race, within any much larger population does not support the proposition that racism is systemic within that population. And it certainly does not justify or excuse painting an entire population as racist. The fact that a criminal of color is injured or killed by an officer of a different color is not evidence of racism. White officers will just as quickly use potentially injurious or deadly force against a white criminal whose behavior warrants it. It just doesn't get the same over-the-top media coverage when they do. Regardless of their color, the overwhelming majority of people injured or killed by police officers started that ball rolling by committing crimes, fleeing, resisting arrest, or refusing to obey the lawful commands of officers. The people who try to support the charge of systemic racism do so by using correlation statistics. Correlation statistics are an inherently flawed foundation upon which to build any argument. Correlation research does not rely on scientific methodology and hypothesis. It only measures two variables and assesses the statistical relationship between them. It does not consider other relevant factors. The nature of law enforcement makes cops the most visible convenient lightning rod for accusations of racism.

"Black Lives Matter" is the current mantra chanted by people who promote the systemic racism lie. That mantra is mindlessly echoed by the critics described in the first part of this work. The critics don't actually believe the mantra. They only use it as a virtue signaling device. "Black lives matter" is not an objective scientific axiom. It is a subjective philosophical proposition. Those who most zealously promote the proposition, and who demand that everyone else accept it as an axiom, do so without objectively defending it. I'm not saying that black lives don't matter. They do matter. And I can defend the proposition better than any of the critics I've heard chanting it. But black lives are no more or less intrinsically valuable than any other lives. It is paradoxical that the people who chant "black lives matter" the loudest are the people who treat black lives with the most abject contempt. If one were to believe the black lives matter narrative, one would think that white police officers patrol the streets for no other reason than to look for innocent black people to harass. That belief would be laughable if it was not so absurd. You have to be a very disturbed person to truly believe that white police officers enjoy seeing any people suffer because of skin color. Try to imagine the thousands of white officers climbing into their cruisers at the beginning of their tour of duty and thinking to themselves, "Hmmm? What would I like to do today? Enjoy a hot cup of coffee under a shady tree while I run some radar? Arrest a drunk driver? Try to locate that missing runaway? Or drive through the hood and have someone I don't even know yell, "Fuck you cracker mother fucker!" as they hurl a rock, a bottle, or a bullet at my cruiser? Gee. I'm feeling especially stupid today, so I think I'll pick option four. Sounds silly, doesn't it? But that appears to be what the BLM crowd thinks. Other than the embarrassingly silly suggestion that we enjoy it, I've yet to hear any of them explain what possible personal or professional benefit they think we would derive from intentionally harassing or harming law abiding people for no reason other than their skin color. It makes no sense. Cops interact with people, regardless of color, when those people do something to initiate the interaction; such as violate the law or call to request help from police. The law abiding people in predominantly black communities are entitled to the same law enforcement services that people in any other community are entitled to. Any reservation a white officer might have about patrolling those communities has nothing to do with the color of its residents. It has to do with the culture. Cops simply want people of every race, ethnicity, and culture to obey the laws of the land and to respect the rights of others to live in peace and safety. Since nearly every black community in America has a street named after Dr. Martin Luther King, one might think that the people in those communities held Dr. King in high regard. I don't believe that they do.

In 1963 Dr. King delivered his famous "I have a dream" speech. In that speech he said: "I have a dream that my four little children will one day live in a nation where they will not be judged by the color of their skin, but by the content of their character."

The overwhelming majority of cops agree with that sentiment. But the only meaningful way cops can evaluate the content of any person's character, regardless of skin color, is by the quality of the person's conduct. And what does rioting, burning, looting, and destroying the property of others say about a person's character? What does giving aid and refuge to criminals who are being sought by police say about a person's character? Here's another notable quote from "Some Things We Must Do," an address Dr. King delivered at the Second Annual Institute on Nonviolence and Social Change at Holt Street Baptist Church in Montgomery Alabama in December, 1957.

"Let us be honest with ourselves, and say that we, our standards, have lagged behind at many points. Negroes constitute ten percent of the population of New York City, and yet they commit thirty-five percent of the crime. St. Louis, Missouri: the Negroes constitute twenty-six percent of the population, and yet seventy-six percent of the persons on the list for aid to dependent children are Negroes. We have eight times more illegitimacy than white persons. We've got to face all of these things. We must work to improve these standards. We must sit down quietly by the wayside, and ask ourselves: 'Where can we improve?'"

Does that offend you? Don't blame me. Take it up with Dr. King. Instead of assuming that white cops are racists, the good people in black communities should be helping us protect them and their communities by supporting our efforts to get the bad guys (and gals) out of those communities. But all too often too many of those otherwise "good people" refuse to assist us. That's not idle speculation. That's a fact that nearly every seasoned officer, black or white, is aware of. Again, it isn't a matter of color. It's a matter of culture. And white virtue signaling hypocrites who are so quick to proclaim the moral and ethical equivalence of all cultures are even quicker to change their tune when the demographics of their own community or personal space begins to shift in a direction that is outside of their personal cultural comfort zone.

During my career I patrolled Asian, Hispanic, and Muslim communities. My presence in those communities was either ignored, politely accepted, or openly appreciated. I never patrolled a Hispanic community and heard someone yell, "Fuck you Gringo!" Or driven through an Asian community and heard someone yell, "Fuck you Gweilo!" Or driven through a Muslim community and heard someone yell, "Fuck you Infidel!" But I can't count the number of times I've driven through African-American communities, both on duty in uniform and off duty in my personal vehicle and heard, "Fuck you cracker mother fucker!" Usually the person hurling that epithet had never met me and didn't even know me. He or she simply hated me because I was white. In case you forgot, that's called "Racism." The rationalizations used to try to excuse that racism are morally and intellectually vacuous. You can rationalize it from now until Kingdom come; it's still racism. And when Kingdom does finally come, as it most certainly will, the person who launched the epithet will not get a race-based pass. They will share the same condemnation and damnation as any other racist. I worked in black communities that were predominantly populated by West Indies immigrants. I easily developed rapport and mutual respect with the people in those communities. Developing a similar rapport in a community of African Americans who were born here and who grew up in hood culture was noticeably more difficult. So it clearly is not about color. It's about culture.

The accusation that white police officers are racists has been made so carelessly and frequently that the accusation now has about as much buying power as a German mark had in 1923. The accusation coming out of the mouth of a high school dropout who makes their living as a drug dealer or as a prostitute isn't a surprise. But the accusation is more troubling when it comes out of the mouth of a highly educated black person who knows better, but who makes the accusation because it is less embarrassing than taking responsibility for their own poor judgment that caused them to have an unpleasant encounter with an officer. Being hostile towards an officer who is simply doing his job doesn't help. But we understand that people sometimes have personal stresses that cause them to have a momentary lapse of judgment during the encounter.

Most cops would graciously forgive that hostility if the person displaying it would just take a moment to realize their foolishness and offer a simple apology with a brief explanation such as, "Sorry officer. I had a bad day at work," or "Sorry officer. I just had an argument with my spouse," or "Sorry officer. My kid just got suspended from school for fighting," etc. would go a long way towards deescalating a stressful encounter. Those stressors are things that most officers can personally relate to, so they can offer sympathy and an olive branch to someone who is big enough to apologize and explain their momentary lapse of judgment. But when the person the officer is righteously confronting doubles down by denying their own culpability and accuses the officer of being motivated by racism, that will not buy them any sympathy or understanding.

Several illustrations come to mind. One of them is the 2009 arrest of Harvard Professor Dr. Henry Gates by Cambridge Police Sergeant James Crowley. I've read the report and the probable cause affidavit. Crowley responded to a 911 call that someone appeared to be burglarizing what turned out to be Gates' home. Neither the caller nor Crowley personally knew Gates. When Crowley arrived, he discovered Gates inside the home. Crowley's responsibility at that point was to investigate to ensure that the home had not been burglarized and that Gates had a lawful right to be in the home. The report indicates that Gates became argumentative and uncooperative without any justifiable provocation. Instead of providing the information that would have allowed Crowley to satisfactorily conclude the investigation and be on his way, Gates pulled the race card. According to the report, he began yelling and calling Crowley a racist police officer. He repeated the accusations several times during the encounter. Gates' loud and aggressive hostility was allegedly witnessed by multiple people. It finally resulted in Crowley arresting Gates for disorderly conduct. Some of Gates' remarks, as detailed in the report, sound more like comments that would come from the mind and mouth of a street thug rather than from the mind and mouth of a well-educated and highly respected PhD. professor. To add insult to injury, President Obama weighed in on the issue by saying "Police acted stupidly."

He would have done better to have said nothing at all. Or if a reporter asked him for a comment and he felt that he had to say something, he should have said, "I was not there. It is inappropriate for a sitting president to comment on a misdemeanor arrest within a municipality that he does not reside in. And you're an idiot for asking the question." Well, duh! How difficult was that? It took me about twenty seconds to come up with it.

Here are a few of his other comments: ". . .you probably don't need to handcuff a guy, a middle-aged man who uses a cane, who's in his own home." It isn't about need. It's about policy. Most law enforcement agencies have a policy that people who violate a criminal statute in an officer's presence are to be arrested, handcuffed and searched for weapons. There is no exemption based on age, race, or sex. Any physical disability that an arrested person has that might cause an officer to violate that policy would need to be substantial and documented in the associated event report. An officer who takes someone into custody, but does not cuff the person, is responsible for any harm the person does if that harm would have been prevented by being cuffed per department policy. It should not be assumed that a middle aged professor with a PhD and a cane is not capable of doing harm, especially if he had a verbally uncooperative attitude. Among the president's other comments were that it didn't make sense to him that the situation escalated to the point that Gates was arrested. Perhaps the president should have asked Gates why he unnecessarily escalated the situation. The president said, "I think that I have extraordinary respect for the difficulties of the job that police officers do."

He also said, ". . . my suspicion is that words were exchanged between the police officer and Mr. Gates and that everybody should have just settled down and cooler heads should have prevailed." Obama's narcissism is off the charts. Cooler heads usually do prevail when both parties are cool headed. But when one person is cool headed and the other person is an argumentative hothead, the hothead sets the tone and things tend to go south. The president's suspicions are irrelevant. If the president understood, as he claimed to, that Crowley was an "outstanding police officer," that was all the more reason for him to avoid commenting on the event. But he could not seem to keep his mouth shut. So he added that with all that's going on in the country with health care and the economy and the wars abroad, "it doesn't make sense to arrest a guy in his own home if he's not causing a serious disturbance." An officer is supposed to make decisions based on state statutes as those statutes apply to the immediate circumstances that the officer is dealing with; not on health care, the economy, and wars abroad. But the president's narcissism compelled him to reinterpret a simple local misdemeanor arrest within his own sphere of responsibility. That is the essence of narcissism: "It's all about me!" What did the subject matter experts have to say?

Cambridge Police Department Commissioner Robert C. Haas said, "I believe that Sgt. Crowley acted in a way that's consistent with his training and national standards," and "I don't believe in any way that his actions were racially motivated."

"Based on what I have seen, he maintained a professional decorum through the entire situation and maintained himself in a professional manner."

Sgt. Tom Fleming, director of the Lowell Police Academy, characterized Crowley as "a squared away guy" and "a really good role model for young cops."

Alan McDonald, the lawyer for the Cambridge Police Superior Officers Association, said Obama "was dead wrong to malign this police officer specifically and the department in general."

Crowley said that the president's characterization was "way off base" and "I acted appropriately." Crowley also made the observation that I already pointed out. He said, "I think he's way off base wading into a local issue without knowing all the facts, as he himself stated before he made that comment. Mr. Gates was given plenty of opportunities to stop what he was doing. He didn't. He acted very irrational. He controlled the outcome of that event." Crowley said Gates called him a "racist cop." "There was a lot of yelling, there was references to my mother," "something you wouldn't expect from anybody that should be grateful that you were there investigating a report of a crime in progress, let alone a Harvard University professor." But here is a fact that people on both sides of the issue seem to miss. The attention given to a simple misdemeanor arrest in a suburban metropolitan municipality illustrates the tactics that the mainstream media and race-baiting politicians use to create divisive strife within a population.

Of course Professor Gates' account of the incident differs from Sgt. Crowley's and other witnesses. Who are you going to believe? If you presuppose that Crowley and the witnesses are conspiratorial liars, and that Gates personal integrity is beyond reproach, you will probably believe Gates. If you have no presuppositions, and if you take the undisputed portions of the report and the circumstances of the encounter at face value, you will probably believe Crowley. Professionally speaking for myself, Crowley's report has a dispassionate and accurate tone to it, so I'm inclined to believe it. You might say, "How do you know! You weren't there!" That's true. I was not there. But Crowley's account of the events had some amazing similarities to an encounter that I had with a black PhD. college professor more than twenty years earlier. Of course you can say, "We weren't there. Why should we believe you?" Because, unlike Crowley, I have an audio recording of a substantial portion of that encounter. I also have a video recording showing the professor being verbally combative and uncooperative with myself and a civilian sheriff's employee while we were being exceedingly patient and respectful with him. Here is an account of that incident.

In the summer of 1987, I was working the 11 P.M. to 7 A.M. shift as a Deputy Sheriff in Broward County, Florida. At approximately 1:30 A.M., I and two other deputies (Jim and Ray) responded to a resort hotel in the City of Lauderhill. A hotel employee called 911 to report that an intoxicated male guest had just climbed into a car in the hotel parking lot and was about to drive away. The employee gave no other information about the man or the car. The other deputies and I were nearby, so we all arrived at the hotel within a minute of being dispatched. Each of us drove down a different parking aisle to look for the man and the car. As I drove down one of the aisles, I saw the brake lights on a car briefly illuminate and then go dark. I stopped behind the car and I advised dispatch. I walked up to the driver's side of the car. The windows were so darkly tinted that I could not see who or what was in the car. When I tapped on the driver's window, the driver's door opened. Sitting behind the wheel was a heavy set black male in his mid-forties. He was wearing unbuttoned and unzipped tuxedo trousers, a disheveled tuxedo shirt and dress shoes. His alcohol laden breath wafted from the open doorway. I said, "Good evening sir."

He said "Hey, how ya doin?"

Since he was obviously intoxicated, I politely said "You're not planning on driving anywhere are you?"

He said "No, no. I just came out to get something out of my car."

By this time, Jim reached my location, looked at the man and said, "Is that you doc?"

The man replied, "Hey, how ya doin?"

Jim said to me, "Do you know who this is?"

I had never seen the man before, so I said "No."

Jim said, "That's Doctor Joyner, the criminal law instructor at the Broward Police Academy." I later learned that the Joyner held a Juris Doctorate Degree from a university in another state.

Ray (the other deputy) arrived at our location and said, "Hey doc. What's going on?" Obviously, Ray also recognized Joyner. After a brief discussion, the three of us agreed that Joyner was too intoxicated to drive. We offered to call a taxi for him or get one of his friends to take him home. He refused the offer. As a professional courtesy we even offered to personally drive him home in one of our cruisers. He also declined that offer. He exited his car and walked back to a hotel ballroom that was occupied by about a hundred formally dressed black guests. A hotel employee told us the gathering was a function related to the United Negro College Fund. We located several guests who knew Joyner. We explained Joyner's condition and our concern for his safety. We asked them to keep an eye on him to prevent him from driving. They assured us that they would. No crime had been committed, so there was nothing else for us to do. Jim and Ray left the hotel property to resume patrol. I had a traffic crash report to finish, so I parked at the hotel entrance to take advantage of a very bright street light there. In addition to giving me the light I needed to finish my report, the bright street light also caused the reflective green stripes and gold star on the side of my cruiser to glow like a Christmas tree. I hoped my highly visible presence would discourage any intoxicated guests from driving from the hotel. Approximately twenty minutes later, the employee who made the original complaint approached me and told me that the same man we encountered earlier had just entered a car and was about to drive away. I told the employee that I would take whatever law enforcement action was appropriate, regardless of who the man was. At that very moment, Joyner drove by my cruiser and looked me dead in the eye as he headed toward the exit. I followed him onto Inverrary Boulevard to watch his driving pattern. He nearly struck the curb of the median numerous times and he repeatedly drifted over the lane dividing line. That, coupled with my previous contact with him, gave me more than enough probable cause to stop him. I radioed to Jim and asked him to head my way as back-up before I initiated the stop. Jim was about two minutes away. About thirty seconds later, Joyner turned onto the county's largest and most heavily traveled roadway. The potential for a traffic crash became too great to let him continue, so I activated my emergency lights and stopped him.

I walked up to his window and said, "Good evening sir. May I see your license and registration please?"

He replied, "You know who I am."

I said, "Yes sir, but I still need to see your license and registration."

He got out of his car and angrily said, "This is a hassle!" as he walked to the rear of his car and opened the trunk. The trunk contained a tuxedo jacket and a tall rectangular briefcase of the type often used by attorneys. It had two overlapping top flaps that were secured by two latches. Joyner gave me a long hard stare, alternating his attention between my eyes, my upper body and my pistol. I had seen that look countless times during my career. It's called "target glancing." It's what someone does to assess an officers mental and physical vulnerability, and it is frequently a prelude to a sudden violent attack. Joyner turned his attention to the brief case. He turned the latches and lifted the flaps. There was a yellow folded towel laying on top of whatever was inside the case. Since I couldn't see what was under the towel, I considered the possibility that the case contained a weapon. I took a step back, wrapped my fingers tightly around the grip of my pistol, and unsnapped the retention strap as I closely watched Joyner's hands. Joyner heard the snap of my holster's retention strap. He stopped and repeated the target glancing as before. He then closed the flaps and secured the latches without lifting the towel or taking anything from the case. He picked up his tuxedo jacket and handed me his driver's license from one of the pockets. I told him that his driving pattern caused me concern that he might be impaired. I asked him to take a roadside sobriety test so I could assess his fitness to drive.

He replied, "I ain't gonna take no fuckin test for you!" That was when Jim arrived. I walked back to Jim and told him that Joyner was being uncooperative. I suggested that, since they were already acquainted, Joyner might be more cooperative with him.

After a polite appeal by Jim, Joyner said, "Alright! I'll take your fuckin test!" I showed Joyner several simple coordination and reflex exercises that police officers commonly use to evaluate a person's level of impairment. I then asked him to do the exercises. He failed all of them, and not by a small margin. I put my left hand on his upper right arm and I told him that I was arresting him for driving while impaired. He physically stiffened, pulled away and said, "You ain't arrestin me!" I grabbed his arm again as he continued to struggle. Jim grabbed his left arm to help me control him. He continued to pull away and repeatedly refused my instruction to stop resisting and to put his hands behind his back. When I told him that I was going to charge him with resisting arrest, he reluctantly allowed me to cuff him and seat him in the back seat of my car. Since his car was in the roadway, and no one was available to drive it from the scene, I radioed for dispatch to send a wrecker to tow it. While I sat in my car to complete some paperwork, Jim assisted me by doing a vehicle inventory / towing report. I kept a small cassette recorder in my car to take statements and to protect myself from potential false allegations by people I arrested. I pressed the record button. What follows is a transcript of what was captured in that recording. What appear to be typographical errors are precise dialog and phonetic spellings:

> **Joyner:** You know I didn't do anything wrong and you stopped me. And I took all my talent to train you… I was very impartial… I have never been a prejudice person mother fucker. But from this day forward I will hate you mother fuckers till the day I die, and if I had a gun I'd blow your fuckin brains out right now. So I don't ever want to teach at the criminal justice institute again.

> **Me:** (calling from my window to Jim) Jim! Jim! Just so you'll know, he just told me that if he had a gun he'd blow my fuckin brains out right now.

> **Joyner:** I didn't say nothin. You're a scum o'the earth. Ya fuckin shit-ass.

> **Me:** Mr. Joyner….

> **Joyner:** (interrupting me) You're a sucker, ya know that? I used to think that people judged people by their own qualities and what they… what… the purities of the individual. But I see you're just a prejudice mother fucker to the mere fact that I'm black.

> **Me:** (to dispatch) Six-o-eight (608 was my unit designation that evening).

Dispatch: One alpha six-o-eight.

Me: Advise ten-fifty time and ten-fifteen reference signal one.

Dispatch: Ten-fifty at two-twenty-seven.

Me: Twenty-six. Case number and ten-fifteen?

Dispatch: Fifty-four advising ten-fifteen. Standby for case… … Case number 2368.

Me: Ten-four. Show me fifteen at two-forty-two.

Dispatch: Ten-four.

Joyner: Fuckin shit-ass mother fucker. A fuckin no good son-of-a-bitch cracker like you. You ain't shit, you know that? And I'm gonna sue your fuckin ass too. First of all you didn't have probable cause to stop me. You have turned my whole philosophy of life. I will hate every fuckin cracker I see from this day forward as a result of your fuckin behavior. [while this conversation was occurring, Jim opened the trunk of Joyner's car to inventory the contents. Joyner's car was about ten feet directly in front of my cruiser, so Joyner could see what Jim was doing.

Joyner: (yelling at Jim. Jim can't hear him) Hey! Hey! Hey pig! You don't have a right to look in my fuckin car! (to me) Hey! He ain't got a right to look in my car! Hey! Hey!

[A few moments later I heard Jim yell my name. I looked up from my paperwork. Jim was standing at the trunk of Joyner's car. He stood facing me so I could see what he was doing. With his right hand, he lifted the flaps of the briefcase, stuck his hand under the towel, and pulled out a model 19 Smith & Wesson .357 magnum revolver with a four inch barrel and six rounds of .357 magnum hollow-point ammo. I then realized that Joyner was planning to kill me when we were at his trunk. The only thing that stopped him from attempting it was my obvious heightened state of preparedness.]

Joyner: You're a fuckin creep, ya know that? You're a fuckin ass racist ass mother fuckin creep. And I'm gonna have to sue your fuckin ass to the bone. And I'm gonna have your ass kicked off the force, because you're a fuckin.... You didn't have probable cause to stop me number one. And then when you come up there... I passed the sobriety test. You're a fuckin racist. You're the kind of mother fucker that makes the God Damn world go counteractive.

[At this point in the recording, underneath Joyner's remarks, I can be heard advising dispatch that I was leaving the location of the traffic stop and was going to the mobile blood alcohol testing unit.]

Joyner: When I spent all my time and effort tryin' to train police officers to utilize the letter of the law, and you come up here like a fuckin ass son-of-a-bitch you. You make me regurgitate. I hate your mother fuckin ass, and I'm gonna get ya. I'm gonna get ya for this. Don't think you'll get away with this. I'm gonna get your fuckin ass racist ass for this. Fuckin ass scum ass mother fucker you. Shit ass mother fuckin racist fuck... why don't you... you don't... you don't even deserve to be on in law enforcement, you know that? People of your mentality don't even need to be on the street, because you need to just carry a KKK flag and walk the fuckin streets. Cause you don't enforce the law. You just assert your fuckin racist attitude toward blacks, you fuckin fuckin ass mother fucker you. I could knock the fuckin head off you. If I ever get ya again, I'll get ya. You ain't gonna stay on. I bet your ass won't be on the force one fuckin month after you book me. You wanna bet, you son-of-a-bitch you? You fuckin ass cracker. You don't have enough guts to be a man and assert your fuckin racist attitude. You just gotta fuck with people under the rubric of you enforcing the law. You're a fuckin punk. A fuckin ass punk. Anybody that can't be a man and say okay I hate niggers so I'm gonna fuck with niggers... you gotta do it under the rubric of enforcing the law, because you ain't got enough god-damn guts to be a man of your own convictions. You fuckin fagot. I wish I could kick your fuckin teeth out. I'm gonna get your mother fuckin ass, remember that, okay? You gonna pay for this bitch. Fuckin fagot mother fucker. You got a pussy. Fuck your pussy. I'm gonna get your ass for this. I swear as long as I live I'm gonna get your fuckin ass you fuckin racist mother fucker. If I ever have to teach another fuckin… I will never teach another… because if they let mother fuckin scum like you… it ain't even worth the effort. And I been bustin my balls researching, studying, to try to teach these people the letter of the law, and tell them that, hey, you don't… your primary responsibility is enforce… you don't let… factors such as race or creed, as long as the law is there. You're just a fuckin ass shit-ass. You don't even deserve to wear a fuckin badge. You know that? You don't… you're not even represented… you're not the type of people that they even throwin a badge on. You a fuckin… you slid under for some reason. You're not a law enforcement officer… you a fuckin racist that hide behind a fuckin badge to permeate your fuckin racist god-damn attitude. If you god-damn it was a man, you'd take off the badge and put on a KKK god-damn hood and do it that way. Don't do it behind a fuckin badge. That fuckin badge has fuckin honor. It has nobility. It's a noble fuckin profession, and scum like you don't even belong in law enforcement god-damn fuckin… you fuckin shit-ass you. I wanna kick your fuckin teeth out you fuckin… fuckin fagot mother fuckin… fagot fuckin god-damn pervert. Under the rubric of the bradge… the badge… you permeate your racist attitude rather than be a law enforcement officer and apply the laws equally regardless of race, creed, color or national origin. You ain't a fuckin law enforcement officer. You a fuckin fagot that ain't got enough god-damn guts to do it on your own accord, but you wanna do it behind a fuckin badge. You a shit-ass you … why don't you take that fuckin uniform off… you don't deserve to wear it. And if I have anything to do with it you won't wear that mother fucker for long. Not for fuckin one month longer than you fuck with me.

Me: (on the radio in response to dispatch asking for my location.) Oakland Park and Third.

Joyner: I wish I would have had you in my class. I would have kicked your fuckin ass out the day I saw you. You fuckin shit-ass fuckin fagot. Under the rubric of the bradge… badge… because you don't have enough guts to do it on your own. You're not a law enforcement officer. You know what you are? A fuckin racist that don't have enough guts to wear the

KKK god-damn, so you use the fuckin badge instead. A fuckin shit-ass fuckin fagot mother fucker. You ain't a law enforcement officer mother fucker. So don't ever tell anybody you are. You a fuckin racist mother fucker who don't have enough guts to permeate your god-damn ideology under the hood of a KKA, so you put on a badge and say I'm enforcing the law. You're a fuckin… fuckin… I'm gonna get your fuckin ass mother fucker, so you might as well beware of it. I'm gonna wear your fuckin ass out. You ain't shit. You ain't shit. You're not a law enforcement officer. Law enforcement officer do not exhibit that type of behavior. It's a noble profession. And scum like you… you probably can't even write your fuckin name mother fucker. Law enforcement officer. How can you call yourself a law enforcement officer? A law enforcement officer enforce the law equably regardless of a person's creed. If he breaks the law, he enforce the law. He doesn't use that fuckin badge to permeate his racist attitude and mentality… and you know god-damn well you didn't have probable cause to stop me mother fucker. And I passed the sobriety test. You just… you use that badge to permeate your racist attitude because you ain't got enough guts to do it as a fuckin man. And I'm gonna fuck you mother fucker. You watch me mother fucker. I'm gonna sue your fuckin ass to the bone. And I'll blow your fuckin brains out on top of it. Because I'm gonna get ya. You don't know who you fucked with tonight, do ya. Obviously ya don't. Racist mother fucker. Why don't you be a man and just wear your KKK hat and do it that way. Why don't you… why do you hide behind a badge to permeate your racist attitude? You ain't shit mother fucker. Any mother fucker like that able to mother fuck… you ain't… you should wear a fuckin skirt you fuckin fagot. Fuckin fagot ass mother fucker. Ain't got a god-damn nough nerve… if I was a racist, you know what I'd do? I'd be a racist and I would say hey, unequivocally of a fuckin racist, I hate blacks, I hate Jews, I hate… I wouldn't hide behind a bladge and say I'm enforcing the law… it's not that I'm racist… I'm just enforcing the law… you fuckin shit-ass mother fucker you. I oughta kick your fuckin teeth out mother fucker. If I ever get out of this car I'll beat your mother fuckin ass. Take these cuffs off me and take me like a man you mother fucker. [Underneath

Joyner's remarks I can be heard advising dispatch of my arrival at the blood alcohol testing unit.] Take me like a man you suckin-stink mother fucker you. Take me like a man you stink shit-ass racist mother fuckin fagot. You ain't shit. Pull off that badge. You don't even deserve to wear a fuckin badge. I train police officers, and if I had seen a fuckin shit-ass like you, I'd have blew your fuckin brains out from the beginning. You hide behind a badge because you ain't got man enough to verbalize your convictions on your own accord. You're a fuckin ass shit-ass.

[At this point we arrived at the mobile blood alcohol testing unit. I stopped the recording temporarily while we were out of the car to conduct that part of the investigation, most of which was captured on video tape. The breath technician was a civilian employee named Harry Conti. What follows is the resumption of my recording Joyner's remarks when we returned to my car so I could complete the arrest affidavit and transport Joyner to jail. There is some brief business related conversation between me and Conti in the background.]

Joyner: I will never teach another police officer. Not even to tie strings in his shoes. You know that? As a result of your fuckin behavior. I will never teach em how to tie a string in his shoe.

Me: (to dispatch) Six-o-eight.

Dispatch: One alpha six-o-eight?

Me: What was my fifty-one and ninety-seven time at BAT?

Dispatch: Ten-fifty-one at three hundred hours, ten-ninety-seven at three-o-nine.

Me: (to dispatch) Twenty-six. (to Conti as he handed me some paperwork) Thanks.

Joyner: (to Conti) Thanks Pompano. (Pompano was the city where we were at the time.)

Conti: See ya doc.

Joyner: (to me) Racist mother fucker. You know what; you're the type of mother fucker that makes this world stand still.

Because of your fuckin god-damn mental attitude towards people that are different than you, and you've abused the god-damn the rights and authority of a badge to permeate your fuckin racist attitudes. Why don't you be a man and just join the KKK and wear a fuckin hood. Why you gotta hide behind a badge mother fucker? You ain't got enough guts? That's what it is. You ain't got enough fuckin guts to be a man. If I was a racist, I wouldn't hide behind a badge to permeate those fuckin attitudes. I would join the KKA and outwardly vocalize my fuckin dissatisfaction discontentment. You fucked up the whole god-damn law enforcement profession. You know that? You're a fuckin god-damn disgrace to the law enforcement profession. It's mother fuckers like you that need to be eliminated, and I'm gonna do my best to get your fuckin ass eliminated.

Me: (to Joyner) How much do you weigh Mr. Joyner?

Joyner: Two pounds mother fucker. How much your mother fuckin mammy weigh?

Me: About a hundred and twenty.

Joyner: Well I weigh two pounds.

Me: Two? You're a pretty big man. I would guess you weigh about two twenty?

Joyner: Two pounds.

Me: How old are you?

Joyner: Three years old.

Me: Where were you born sir?

Joyner: Mars.

Me: Mars? What state is that in?

Joyner: That's in the... eh... the... eh... the eclisical...that's in the planets. Mars. M-A-R-S.

Me: What's your social security number?

Joyner: Five.

Me: Where do you work?

Joyner: Mars.

Me: Mars? How long have you worked there?

Joyner: Five thousand years.

Me: How long have you lived in Broward County?

Joyner: About five thousand years.

Me: Do you have any scars, marks or tattoos?

Joyner: No.

Me: Do you have any nicknames?

Joyner: No.

Me: What year was your car?

Joyner: I don't know.

Me: (on the radio to Jim) Six-o-six, ten ninety-two.

Jim: Six-o-six going over. (pause to switch channels) Six-o-six on.

Joyner: You trailed me from that fuckin god-damn parking lot and I didn't do anything to warrant you stopping me.

Me: (to Jim) What year was that car.

Joyner: You kiss my ass mother fucker. You make me sick.

Jim: (gives year of vehicle)

Me: (to Jim) Four-door?

Joyner: You ain't shit. You make me regurgitate, you know that? You ain't a law enforcement officer. You a fuckin fagot. You're sickening. That's not what law enforcement is all about, okay? Law enforcement is about enforcing the law equally, regardless of race, creed, color or national origin. If a person breaks the law, then you have a right to enforce it. You don't use your fuckin racist attitude, your racist mentality, to permeate it under the rubrics of the law, okay?

If you're gonna be in law enforcement, be in law enforcement. If you wanna be a KKK, pull off the fuckin uniform and put on a hood and a god-damn fuckin hat and just have a KKK. Don't be a coward and do it under the rubric of a fuckin badge and a gun. I would respect you more if you march down the god-damn street with a hood and a fuckin robe sayin KKK, rather than to do it under the rubric of a badge, because that's a noble profession, and only the creme de la creme suppose to be in it. Not scums like you.

[END OF TRANSCRIPT]

The remainder of the sounds on the tape are road and vehicle noise, and miscellaneous radio traffic. Joyner had no other comments to me beyond this point. If I was the "racist mother fucker" that Joyner accused me of being, it would be fair to wonder why I gave him the break of not adding the resisting arrest charge to the charging document. Or why, after the test at the blood alcohol testing location, as he sat handcuffed in the back seat of my cruiser, like an angry bull with snot and sweat running down his face, I held some tissue for him so he could blow his nose. I then wiped the snot and sweat from his face to restore what little dignity he might have remaining before we got to the jail. A few days later I completed an affidavit charging him with "Corruption by threat against a public servant" (Florida Statute 838.021). I took the affidavit and the cassette tape to the attorney in charge of the public corruption unit of the State Attorney's Office. He read the affidavit. When he listened to the tape, he smiled and said, "Oh yeah. I'll take this case." A warrant was issued and Joyner was arrested a few days later. He bonded out of jail. The college placed him on paid administrative leave pending court disposition, but they didn't terminate him. Ray, one of the deputies who responded to the original call, personally knew the academy director, Ed Mandt. He thought it was important that Ed know the details of the event, so he asked me if he could take a copy of the tape to Ed. I gave him a copy of the tape. Ed called me a few days later to tell me that he listened to the tape and that I could come by the college and get the tape at my convenience. When I met with him a few days later to get the tape, I spoke with him for about thirty minutes in his office. He commended me for my professionalism and self-restraint during my encounter with Joyner. He told me that Joyner had been an instructor there for about two and a half years. Ed opened one of his desk drawers and pulled out a file folder that was about a half inch thick with paperwork. He told me that the folder contained various paperwork related to a typical instructor who had been there for about the same amount of time as Joyner. He then pulled out two other folders, each being more than an inch thick and bulging with paperwork. He told me that those folders contained paperwork related to Joyner's employment as an instructor. He told me that much of the paperwork in those folders were complaints from other instructors and students concerning Joyner's argumentative attitude and racial hostility. I asked Ed why he didn't fire Joyner, especially now that he heard the audio tape. Ed explained that he didn't have the authority to fire him because Joyner was a college employee. And since the academy was only part of the college, the only person who could fire him was the college provost. But the provost wouldn't fire him because he, the provost, was fearful of being accused of racism if he did.

If you think that Joyner's behavior and arrest attracted considerable attention from the news media, you're wrong. The text below is from a UPI article that, to the best of my knowledge, is the totality of the news media's coverage of the incident. It's interesting that the journalist who wrote the article was not named and went out of his way to avoid mentioning anything about race or Joyner's racist remarks.

> "June 7, 1987 By United Press International FORT LAUDERDALE — An instructor at Broward County's police academy has been charged with threatening to shoot a deputy sheriff who accused him of drunken driving. Jimmie Joyner, an instructor at the Criminal Justice Institute in Davie, was charged Friday with two counts of felony corruption-by-threat and driving under the influence. Joyner teaches criminal law classes that explain most criminal offenses in Florida, including corruption and drunken driving, institute officials said. Joyner's alleged threats, filled with profanities, were videotaped by equipment in the sheriff's mobile sobriety unit after he was pulled over in Lauderhill last month. "You don't know who you're . . . with tonight," Joyner allegedly told the arresting deputy, Morris Burke. "If I have anything to do with it, you won't wear that . . . uniform for long." And if I had a gun, I'd blow your . . .

brains out right now." Burke said he stopped Joyner, 44, of Pompano Beach, because Joyner's car weaved across the double-yellow line several times. Joyner, if convicted, faces a maximum penalty of 10 years in prison and $10,000 in fines stemming from his threats on Burke and Harry Conti, a sheriff's civilian employee assigned to the sobriety unit. He also is charged with misdemeanor driving while under the influence. He refused to take a breathalyzer test when pulled over. Under state law, refusal to take the test could mean his driver's license will be suspended. Joyner, who holds a law degree from Southern University in Louisiana, has taught at the academy for about three years, said Edward Mandt, the institute's director. Many of Joyner's students are police recruits or veteran law officers returning to school for refresher courses, said Douglas McGregor, chairman of the Department of Criminal Justice Education. Mandt and provost Larry McFarlane said no suspension or other action has been taken against Joyner. McFarlane said he will investigate the case. Joyner was not at the college on Friday and could not be reached for comment. In his report, Burke said while he was parked near a hotel filling out a report, he noticed Joyner drive out of a parking lot onto Inverrary Boulevard. Burke said he followed Joyner and noticed him weaving and nearly hit the curb several times, the report said.' Once stopped, Joyner failed sobriety tests, according to the report. He was unable to consistently touch his nose and could not maintain balance."

[End of Article]

How do you think the news media would have covered the story if I had been a black deputy, Joyner had been a white professor, and the racial epithets were reversed to reflect that difference?

TIPS FOR LAW ABIDING CITIZENS

If you're a law abiding citizen, by now it should be obvious to you that the criminal justice system that you rely on for your safety is broken beyond repair. So here are some tips to help you protect yourself and your loved ones.

In spite of their diligent efforts on your behalf, the amount of protection your law enforcement officers can provide is extremely limited. Most of those limitations come from the judicial and legislative branches of your government. Philosophical elitists in those branches put the comfort of criminals above your safety and well-being. If you have to call us because one of those criminals is endangering your life, and you are unprepared to protect yourself, you will probably be dead before we arrive. And your death will not be a pleasant one. The following anecdote will illustrate my point.

In January of 1995, in a town in central Florida, a 19 year-old high school dropout burglarized the home of an elderly husband and wife by climbing through a bathroom window. Fortunately the husband heard the sound and called the police. Officers arrived. One of them remained outside by the point of entry. The other officer found the male perpetrator still in the bathroom. When that officer confronted the perpetrator, that perpetrator threateningly brandished a screwdriver and took a step towards the officer. When the officer threatened to shoot him, the perpetrator surrendered. They arrested him for armed burglary of an occupied dwelling. Five and a half months later he was sentence to forty-four months in prison. He was released twenty-nine months later, fifteen months before serving his full sentence. He returned to the community where he committed the burglary that sent him to prison. Twenty-three days after his release, at two o'clock in the morning, he climbed through the bathroom window of a seventy-six year-old widow who lived alone. He sexually assaulted her in her bed. He then got her out of bed, and took her car keys and the money from her handbag. He forced her into the trunk of her car that was parked in her carport. He drove away in her car and spent the next ten hours trying to figure out where to dispose of her. He finally drove to a large commercial orange grove in a remote part of an adjoining county. She was still alive. He took her out of the trunk and tried to lead her into the grove, but she was too weak to walk. When she fell down, he dragged her by her ankles about a hundred feet into the grove. He stood her up and tried to kill her by twisting her head to break her neck. When that failed, he pushed her onto her back and recovered a fire extinguisher from the trunk of her car. He stuck the nozzle in her mouth and discharged some of the extinguisher contents. When she didn't immediately die, but lay there gasping and choking, he recovered the tire iron from the trunk. He stuck the bladed end of the tire iron in her mouth and shoved it through the back of her throat until it came out the back of her neck just below the base of her skull. That broke her neck and she died moments later. He then left her body laying in the orange grove and drove away in her car. His identity was discovered within hours and he was arrested that evening. He eventually confessed and gave a statement to officers. He was indicted, tried, convicted, and sentenced to death. As of today, he is still alive. He will probably outlive me and many of you.

As I alluded to earlier, your safety and welfare today are determined by the situational ethics and values of twenty-first century liberal politicians, judges, and lawyers who live well beyond your means and who have no skin in the game. The philosophical gymnastics and convoluted rationalizations these people use to justify the decisions that cops are legally bound to abide by create a labyrinth of confusion that even the politicians, jurists and lawyers who make those decisions could not navigate if their lives depended on it. Lawyers and judges kick cases back and forth for years before a final decision is reached. What you as citizens need to keep in mind is that many of the jurists and lawyers in this chain of challenges are arrogant agnostics who think they have ascended to a higher plane of existence than you. They honestly believe that their enlightened apotheosis entitles them to look down at you as ignorant unwashed masses who need their guidance to survive. To give the devil his due, these guys and gals can be very persuasive in their hundred dollar haircuts, thousand dollar designer suits, hundred thousand dollar European sedans, and million dollar homes. But their legal arguments and opinions are usually theoretical and philosophical psychobabble that has no positive effect on the negative realities that you have to deal with every day. A few years ago, another officer and I were having lunch with a state prosecutor that we knew. Since I was recently retired, it was safe for me to express my opinion without fear of retribution. I told him that I thought the criminal justice system was "a farce."

To my surprise, he agreed with me. He said, "It's just theater. The lawyer who gives the best performance wins the case." That's a pretty damning indictment from someone who knows.

If you're wondering what this has to do with you, the law abiding citizen, consider this: When the lawyers and judges go home at the end of the day, and recidivist defendants, who were as guilty as sin itself, have their cases dismissed, or are given probation for the umpteenth time instead of prison, it won't be the politicians, judges, or lawyers whose homes are burglarized and whose families are terrorized by the recidivists. It will be your homes and your families. Cops can't be everywhere at once. So the odds of us being able to intervene before you or your loved ones become victims are slim to none. With that in mind, you are ultimately responsible for the safety of yourself and your loved ones. If you're wondering how to do that, here are a few general suggestions that should get you off to a good start. This is just a start. The subject of personal safety could fill a separate book or hours of YouTube videos. There are good books and videos out there on the subject. You would be wise to study a few of them. Keep in mind that my suggestions will be roundly condemned by many politicians, judges and lawyers, as well as many high ranking police administrators. Those officials might tell you that I'm wrong, or that following my advice will put you in danger. They don't believe that. The real reason they tell you that is they are concerned that it could jeopardize their power and status when you realize that you can protect yourself better than they can. If you stop relying on them for help, they will be hard pressed to justify their existence. Anyway, here are my suggestions.

1. **Spend some time learning the statutes of your state.** Obviously you can't learn them all. So start with the statutes related to crimes against persons. That would be things like murder, rape, robbery, aggravated assault, battery, stalking, etc. Then learn the laws related to self-defense and the use of force. Then learn the statutes related to crimes against property. That would be things like burglary, theft, auto theft, vandalism, and trespassing. When you have a good general understanding of those statutes, and if you don't already own one, buy a gun suitable for personal protection. If you don't have much shooting experience, get some professional training to become proficient in using it accurately, comfortably, and legally. Having a gun that you can't accurately and comfortably use, or using a gun outside of statutory guidelines will cause you more trouble than you bargained for. Get a permit that allows you to carry it concealed, and carry on your person or readily accessible whenever you leave your home. Carry a knife and chemical agent that conforms to your state's legal restrictions, and learn how to use those items for self-defensive purposes. I am not opposed to martial arts training. I encourage it. But criminals target their victims based on obvious weakness and vulnerability. The elderly, physically disabled, cognitively impaired, or people who are just unaware of what is going on around them are most likely to become victims. Most criminals are tougher than the people they target. How often do you hear of athletes or physically imposing people being robbed or beaten up? If you are elderly, aren't physically imposing, or you don't look like you're prepared to deal with whatever comes your way, you're going to be seen as a potential victim.

2. **Have friends and neighbors of like mind who are willing to participate with you in putting that advice into practice**. Organize with those friends and neighbors. Form a community watch group. Train regularly with them to keep your knowledge up to date and your skills honed. It doesn't take that much time or effort. When practical, travel in pairs or groups. Plan your travel in advance. Know the potential hazards of the places you are going and the routes that you have to take to get there while avoiding trouble areas.

3. **Do not get involved in the problems of other people unless their problems are having an immediate negative effect on your life.** If you are going to get involved in their problems, you'd better be prepared to die because that could be the outcome. Even if their problem appears small, it can explode into a big problem before you realize what is happening. By then it might be too late for you to back out. People who have problems and disputes seem to do so habitually. That is because those people have personality disorders or other psychological problems that regularly bring them into conflict with others. Couple that with their dangerous lifestyles and behavior patterns, and you have a recipe for disaster. Those lifestyles and behavior patterns usually go back to their adolescence or teens. About the only thing you can expect from getting involved in their problems is becoming collateral damage. Call the police on their behalf if you need to. Discretely record the event on your cellphone camera if you can. Pay attention so you can be a good witness for the police if needed. But getting involved in the problems and disputes of others, unless necessary to save their life, is generally a terrible idea.

4. **Practice situational awareness.** Always be aware of your surroundings. Look at the people around you and don't be afraid to be judgmental. Look at their cars, clothing, personal hygiene, grooming, tattoos, piercings, etc. The old saying that "You can't judge a book by its cover" is utter nonsense. Tattoos, fashion accessories, bumper stickers, neglected personal hygiene, poor grooming, etc. should be viewed as forms of intentional or unintentional non-verbal communication. They are windows into what is going on inside a person's heart and head. Tattoos of skulls, snakes, scorpions, guns, knives, etc. suggest an unhealthy fascination with violence and death. Ask yourself why someone would want to convey that fascination to total strangers. Bumper stickers and window decals can tell you where a person stands on political or social issues. That will give you an idea of how they are likely to react if you have opposing views and you have to interact with them. Provocative immodest fashions, heavy

makeup, cross-dressing, etc. advertise a person's moral values or mental illness. Nuns do not wear the attire of hookers, and hookers do not wear Nuns' habits. If these, or any other form of non-verbal communication, cause you any instinctive or intuitive discomfort about a person, listen to your instinct and intuition. Stay as far away from that person as you can. If they approach you, go out of your way to avoid them. If they go out of their way to keep approaching you, loudly and clearly tell them to stay away from you and to leave you alone. Will they obey your command? Maybe. But if they don't, at least your loud and clear warning will attract the attention of bystanders. If the person you are concerned about ignores your warnings and continues toward you, prepare to defend yourself. If you have to resort to violence, at least the bystanders will be able to testify that you appeared to be in fear, that you warned the person to leave you alone, and that the person ignored your warning and invaded your personal space. Here is an important warning: If you have "woke" friends or family members who try to bully or shame you into ignoring your instinct and intuition in favor of accepting their "loving" or "open minded" beliefs by calling you "judgmental" or "narrow-minded," cut those people out of your life. Block them from your phone and social media accounts. They will never stop badgering you to convert you to their beliefs. When those beliefs bring chaos into their lives, they will find a way to blame that chaos on you or those who think as you do. In spite of that, they will try to shame you into rescuing them from the chaos because none of their like-minded friends are able to.

5. **Practice home and personal security.** If you see suspicious cars or people in your neighborhood or around your business, discreetly photograph or video record them if you can. Keep a diary of suspicious people, vehicles, phone calls, or events that you observe. You never know if or when your diary entries will be of value at some later date. Keep your doors locked and your window down far enough that someone can't climb through the opening. This applies even if you are home, especially at night. If you want fresh air, there are cheap

gadgets that you can attach to your window frame that will allow you to open your window far enough for some fresh air, but will prevent the window from being opened far enough for anyone to crawl through. Keep your car locked. Don't leave valuables in the passenger compartment where they can be seen. Have motion activated security lights and a security camera system. If you can't afford a real security camera system, there are inexpensive realistic looking counterfeit cameras that you can install around the exterior of your home that will discourage most would-be criminals. Post signs around your property that say, "no trespassing," "property under video surveillance," and "no soliciting." If someone you don't recognize comes on your property, don't be afraid to verbally challenge them from a safe distance. If they make it to your door or window before you see them, they obviously ignored your signs. Consider them a threat and arm yourself. If you cannot see their hands because they have their hands in their pockets or behind their back, or if they are carrying any container that you cannot see the contents of, they are absolutely a threat. Consider asking them in a confrontational tone of voice, "Who are you, and what are you doing on my property?" If they do not immediately give you a reasonable credible explanation for their presence, tell them to get off your property. If they do not immediately leave, or if they become argumentative, call 911 and prepare for war. Leave the line open so the 911 recording system can capture you telling the person to leave. If things go bad, at least the 911 recording system will probably capture enough of it for you to use in your own defense if you have to seriously injure or kill them. Do not share any personal information with people that you don't know, regardless of how legitimate their reason for asking seems to be. There are some very slick scammers out there who can fool all but the smartest of people.

6. **Stop watching violent movies and television shows**. Why? Aside from those programs being spiritually and psychologically toxic, they portray potentially real life situations in a very unrealistic manner. Slow motion, dramatic lighting, exciting background music, closeups

and rapidly changing camera perspectives are all artistic elements that will not be present in a real life crisis or confrontation. Repeatedly viewing those elements in movies and television shows will imprint on your subconscious mind and will become your default expectations should find yourself in a real life crisis or confrontation. Bad things usually happen in a split second, and the results are usually much more calamitous, painful, and long lasting than portrayed in movies and television shows. One good punch from someone can happen in a split second and can be enough to leave you permanently disabled or dead, especially if you are old, or frail, or have a preexisting medical condition. And someone who gets that close to you could launch such a punch so quickly that you would lose consciousness before you could even process that it was on its way. Modern movies and television programs turn lies to truth, and turn truth to lies. They will corrupt your values and grossly distort your perception of reality. Turn that shit off, because that's what it is: Pure unadulterated shit!

TIPS FOR COPS

Since I was so hard on the cop critics, it's only fair that I be as blunt with my brothers by offering some advice to help you physically, mentally and financially survive the job. You don't have to agree with me or abide by my advice. But if you ignore it and something bad happens as a result, at least you can't blame me or say that nobody warned you. Some of this advice is from some old timer colleagues who are wiser than me. Some of it is based on foolish mistakes I made during my own career. So take advantage of our experiences.

This first tip isn't going to sit well with some of you; especially if you're an overly ambitious administrator or a brainwashed young rookie. If you fall into either of those categories, you need to take a long hard look in the mirror and reevaluate your professional and personal priorities. Here's the tip. Always keep in mind that you work for either a municipal, a county, or a state government agency for the welfare of the people of your municipality, county, or state. You don't work for the federal government. So don't salivate like a Pavlovian dog whenever agents from alphabet federal agencies (FBI, ATF, etc.) show up. They are not movie stars. They are not smarter or more talented than you are. They are not ethically or morally superior to you. Based on the recent performance of many of them, probably less so. They do not work for the people in your community. They work for a corrupt US Department of Justice. The DOJ has become a cudgel used by morally and ethically bankrupt politicians to instill fear in people who don't agree with their views and agenda.

Unless you've been living under a rock for the past few decades, it should be obvious to you that the agenda of those politicians is a global one that is opposed to the ideals expressed in the constitution that you swore to support and defend, and is destructive to the health and safety of the people that you're supposed to protect. Or, as Ronald Reagan so succinctly put it during a 1986 press conference, implicitly referring to the federal government; "The nine most terrifying words in the English language are: I'm from the Government, and I'm here to help." There are some good federal law enforcement officers who agree with my views. They are disgusted with the politicization of their agencies. They hate their supervisors. They despise their agencies' leadership. They loath the politicians who appointed that leadership. And they mistrust their boot-licking coworkers. But they have so much time invested in their careers that they can't afford to bail out. So, they just try to tread water or fly under the radar long enough to retire and collect their pensions. Some of them have begun blowing the whistle on the corruption within their agencies. I wish more of them would. As for you, choose who you want to fight for. The globalists and their federal gestapo? Or for the law abiding people of your state, county, or municipality. You can't do both. They are mutually exclusive.

PEANUT'S PRINCIPLES

When I was a 21 year-old new officer, one of our academy instructors was a captain from my department. He was a nice country gent that his friends called "Peanut." Peanut had a Mayberry-like southern accent and nasal twang that I can still hear reverberating in my memory as I recall the following warning that he gave us during a class on ethics:

> "I'm gonna tell you boys somethin that some a'yall ain't gonna pay attention to. But some a'yall gonna find out the hard way. As a police officer, they's three things that'll get you in trouble every time. Money, whiskey, and women!"

Looking back on my career, I can tell you that Peanut's advice was prophetic. Nearly every officer that I have known (including myself) who got into trouble did so by violating one or more of Peanut's Principles. Some of those officers lost their jobs. Some of them lost their certification and their pensions. Some of them lost their freedom. And a few of them lost their lives. The attitude of many of today's self-centered young rookies and burned-out old veterans is, "What I do on my time is nobody's business!" That claim is so childish that it is hardly worthy of a response. But I'm going to respond anyway.

MONEY

As society decays, the acquisition of wealth has become an obsession for most people. It's more important to them than having self-respect or a good reputation. Cops sometimes fall into that trap. When I first became an officer in the early 1970s, most agencies ran credit checks on officer applicants as part of the background investigation. Applicants who had bad credit, oppressive debt, bankruptcies, or outstanding financial judgments were disqualified. I can hear some of you whining, "That's not fair!" Yes it is, for a number of reasons. If those conditions are not caused by unforeseeable events beyond your control, they are caused by you living beyond your means or by your unwillingness to responsibly manage your financial affairs. That is a direct reflection of your lack of self-discipline or your lack of good judgment. If you cannot or will not responsibly manage your personal finances in a way that prevents you from getting deeply into debt, why should a law enforcement agency trust you with the awesome responsibilities of protecting the lives and property of other people? Officers who are deep in debt or living beyond their means are serious risks for committing thefts, accepting bribes, taking gratuities, or committing fraud. Otherwise honest cops who get into financial trouble will sometimes physically overextend themselves by working off-duty details or side jobs to keep up with their debt. Many agencies have restrictive policies regarding secondary employment. Secondary employment or off-duty security details must be approved by the agency. Off-duty security details are scheduled through the agency to prevent officer fatigue from interfering with on duty performance. Falling asleep or being impaired by fatigue while on duty can be hazardous to your health and to the health of your brother officers. Most of the trinkets you are working so hard to acquire are nothing but status symbols that clever marketers have brainwashed you into thinking that you need. Those trinkets aren't worth dying for. And they certainly aren't worth causing the death of a brother officer. Officers with financial problems are more likely to gamble and become gambling addicts. Whether the gambling is legal or illegal becomes irrelevant. Spending half of your paycheck on lottery tickets is just as foolish as losing half of it in an illegal card game. Organized criminals who know that an officer is in financial trouble will sometimes offer to buy confidential information about department operations or personnel. If the debt is so deep that the officer sees no way of getting out honestly, he'll take the offer. If you wanted to become wealthy, you should have chosen a different line of work. Quit now and find something more profitable. If you like being a cop and you want to keep your job, but you still want to improve your financial state, work hard to achieve a higher rank and pay grade. Save your money and make wise investments.

WHISKEY

"O God, that men should put an enemy in their mouths to steal away their brains! that we should, with joy, pleasance revel and applause, transform ourselves into beasts!"
- Cassio to Iago, Othello, Act II, Scene iii,
by William Shakespeare, 1564 – 1616

"Drunkenness is nothing but a condition of insanity purposely assumed. . . Think of the calamities caused by drunkenness in a nation. This evil has betrayed to their enemies the most spirited and warlike races; this evil has made breaches in walls defended by the stubborn warfare of many years; this evil has forced under alien sway peoples who were utterly unyielding and defiant of the yoke; this evil has conquered by the wine-cup those who in the field were invincible."
- Lucius Annaeus Seneca, Roman Stoic philosopher
and statesman, c. 4 BC- c. 65 AD.

If you're a seasoned officer, think of the calls you answered in which people were killed or injured in alcohol related automobile crashes, boating mishaps, industrial accidents, recreational activities, or personal confrontation. Think of the fortunes lost, families broken, and health destroyed. And yet the consumption of alcohol is promoted by liquor manufacturers who want you to drink as much of their product as possible. Their advertisements portray the consumption of alcohol as manly conduct. Those advertisements are designed to manipulate you into mentally linking their product to your masculinity. The tag line that is heard or printed at the end of those advertisements ("Drink Responsibly) is nothing but psychological manipulation to make you think they care about your well-being. They don't. And neither do your friends and coworkers who try to talk you into joining them in their drunken revelry by mocking you if you don't. The manufacturers only care about what's in your wallet. Your friends and coworkers only care about easing their own wounded consciences by having you share their misery.

At one of the agencies I worked for, the officers on my squad would badger me to join them for "choir practice" in the parking lot when our shift ended at 11 P.M. Choir practice was the term they used for gathering in the parking lot after work to drink beer and complain about their problems, most of which were self-inflicted. One of them would go to a nearby convenience store and pick up a couple of six-packs of beer. He would then bring it back to the parking lot where the officers would stand around drinking and talking for a couple of hours. Since I didn't drink, I didn't sing with the choir. But they continued to badger me. One evening they said, "We'll buy you a soda instead of beer if you'll join us." I caved in. When the officer returned with the beer, he brought me a soft drink. As I stood there, watching them get buzzed and listening to them talk, one of them began whining about how his wife was always complaining that he was never home, that he never talked with her, and that he never took her anywhere.

So I said, "Do you talk to your wife?"

He replied, "Not if I don't have to."

I then said, "Do you ever take her anywhere?"

After thinking for a moment he said, "No." I then pointed out that he had been off-duty for two hours and was standing in a parking lot and drinking beer instead of being with his wife and child at their apartment that was three blocks away. Choir practice ended about a minute later. I was never invited back.

My first job as an officer was at a small city in central Florida. After I completed field training and went solo, one evening my shift sergeant invited me to "Go Lumming" with the rest of the squad when the shift ended at 11 P.M. Lumming was the term they used in reference to going to "Lum's" to talk and drink beer. Lum's was a chain of casual family restaurants known for beer served in frosted mugs and hot dogs steamed in beer. Being the squad's rookie at twenty-one, I figured it was in my best interest to join them. They all ordered beer. I ordered a sweet tea. They insisted that I have a beer with them and told the waitress to bring me a beer and put it on their tab. So the waitress brought me a beer. I soon became aware that they were watching me, hoping I would get drunk. I disappointed them. I only drank about six ounces from the glass. Since I was unaccustomed to drinking alcohol, that was all I needed feel a little buzzed, but not so buzzed that my demeanor changed or my faculties were impaired. I realized that drinking with them was a bad idea, so I said goodnight and headed home. One of those officers became a good friend. He was an exceptionally smart and talented guy. His professional knowledge and investigative skills were amazing. But the daily stresses of the job became so depressing for him that he self-medicated with alcohol. He eventually became a lieutenant. He also became a twice divorced raging alcoholic and had to retire because of several DUI arrests. He died drunk and alone after falling in his bath tub. He suffered from alcohol related dementia, heart problems, and liver damage. He was only 60 years-old.

So, go ahead. Scoff at me. Prove your manliness and social affability by drinking. When you're dying of liver disease, you will have a hard time finding a doctor who is willing to transplant the healthy liver of a recently deceased donor into the abdominal cavity of someone who destroyed their own liver with alcohol. You'll also probably die alone because you will have alienated nearly everyone who truly cared about you.

A large percentage of domestic violence and homicide cases involving police officers are alcohol related in the sense that the officer's judgment was impaired by alcohol. If you find yourself under arrest for DUI, vehicular homicide, domestic battery or some other criminal act because you were impaired by alcohol, it will not be the fault of the officer who arrests you. And it will not be the CEO of a brewery or some Madison Avenue advertising executive who pays your medical bills, posts your bond, pays your attorney, or serves your prison sentence.

Here is a little piece of history to think about. On April 15th, 1865, at approximately 9 P.M., President Abraham Lincoln was attending a play at Ford's Theater in Washington, DC. Officer John Parker of the DC police department was assigned to the post outside Lincoln's private box to protect the President. During intermission, Parker joined the footman and coachman of Lincoln's carriage for drinks at the Star Saloon next door to Ford's Theater. When John Wilkes Booth entered the theater around 10 P.M. and crept up to the door to Lincoln's box, Parker's chair was empty. It isn't clear where Parker was when Booth pulled the trigger. But there is good reason to believe that he was still at the saloon. Parker had a history of drunkenness, including being drunk while on duty.

WOMEN

If you are currently an unmarried or divorced male police officer, or an unmarried or divorced man who wants to become a police officer, I would advise you to remain single. If you are currently married, you have my deepest sympathy. If you are cohabiting, end that situation asap. If you struggle with a proclivity towards sexual promiscuity or deviance, find a different line of work.

Women can provide valuable services within a police agency. Being a uniformed patrol officer is not among those services. In a scene from the 1976 movie, "The Enforcer," Dirty Harry Callahan succinctly highlights the problem. He and several other veteran officers are serving on an oral exam board for officers who have applied for several openings for Inspector. Harry is not pleased when he learns that several of the openings are already earmarked for female officers, regardless of exam performance or board recommendations. The exam is being monitored by Ms. Grey, an estrogen-depleted harridan from the Mayor's staff. She tells Harry that the Mayor, ". . . intends to broaden the areas of participation for women in the police force."

Harry replies, "Well that sounds very stylish Mrs. Grey." Female Officer Moore enters. She admits that her career has been spent in personnel and records and that she has never made an arrest. Harry tells her that, under the Mayor's guidelines, she might be riding in a police car.

She says, "Yes sir that's what I'm hoping for."

Harry angrily asks, "What the hell gives you the right to become an inspector when there's men have been out there on the street for ten or fifteen years?"

During an angry exchange with Gray, Harry says, "What do you think this is some kind of encounter group? I want to know what officer Moore is gonna do when somebody points a gun at her and says hit the deck you son of a Bitch!" Harry points out to Moore that she could get "her ass blown away" on the street.

Moore stoically snaps back, "It's my ass. . . and my hard luck." Harry points out that she'll have a partner and that if she gets blown away, he gets blown away with her.

Harry's last line in the exchange is, "That's a hell of a price to pay for being stylish!" That truth, so eloquently expressed by Harry, happens all too often in real world law enforcement.

If you're a male officer who has to work with female officers, you must resist your natural male instinct to protect them. You must stay sharply focused on your own safety. When a woman becomes a sworn officer, she forfeits any special consideration that she previously enjoyed because of her gender. Never trust your life or your safety to a female officer who is supposed to be backing you up. She was hired to satisfy social, political, and cultural agendas. Her ability to properly do the job and back you up was not and never will be considered. If you happen to be present at a scene where something bad happens as a result of her poor judgment or limitations, you can be sure that the bosses who hired her are going to be looking for a way to throw you under the bus and hold you at least partially responsible for not doing something to prevent it. Why? To absolve themselves of their culpability for hiring her in the first place.

Never establish any romantic or sexual relationship with any female employed in any position in your agency. Never risk your life for a female officer who is expecting you to protect her because she is physically and psychologically ill equipped for the job. She is not worth dying for. Her employment was a unilateral decision by your agency's leadership; a decision over which you had no input or control.

An issue that no one who supports the hiring of female officers wants to talk about is PMS (premenstrual syndrome). While PMS is not recognized as a legal defense in the United States, England and Canada have recognized it as a mitigating factor, and France recognizes it as a form of legal insanity. In the political push towards globalism, it's only a matter of time before the US recognizes it. And while it is not recognized as a legal defense in criminal cases, that does not mean that your boss cannot be bullied into recognizing it as a mitigating factor in administrative or disciplinary consideration. That recognition could cost you dearly. PMS has a wide variety of medically recognized symptoms, including mood swings, food cravings, fatigue, irritability and depression. It's estimated that as many as three of every four menstruating women have experienced some form of premenstrual syndrome. I've personally witnessed those symptoms in female officers. Do you want to put your physical and professional survival in the hands of someone who is, for all practical purposes, physically impaired or insane for several days during the month?

If you are a male field training officer, make it clear to your boss that you will not accept female trainees. If your boss will not allow you to exercise that option, withdraw from your agency's field training program. If your boss tells you that he will not let you opt out, contact a lawyer or your union representative and ask them for help, even if it means taking your boss to court. Is it that serious an issue? Absolutely. Your female trainee's potential for a psychotic meltdown under the kinds of stress she will experience as an officer is significant. If she accuses you of groping her, or sexually propositioning her, or saying something that she finds personally offensive, you will find yourself under internal investigation. If you're married, how do you think that is going to affect your relationship with your wife? And the trainee's accusation doesn't have to be sexual in nature. She can accuse you of saying or doing any number of things that could potentially destroy your career. When a woman lodges any accusation against a man in today's cultural atmosphere, the man is presumed guilty unless he can prove himself innocent beyond a reasonable doubt. And even if her complaint is determined to be unsubstantiated, that is not the same as it being unfounded. If an allegation cannot be proven to be true or false, it will be labeled as unsubstantiated. The stink of an unsubstantiated allegation can remain on you for the rest of your life. It can wreck your marriage, destroy the trust of your coworkers and supervisors, block your career path within the agency, and prevent you from ever being hired by another agency.

Beware of "badge bunnies." For those of you not familiar with the term, badge bunnies are women who are sexually attracted to cops. A police uniform has an almost aphrodisiac effect on some women. No matter how physically attractive they might be to you, those women are mentally ill and should be avoided like the plague. Most badge bunnies collect badges, figuratively speaking, by sleeping with the men who wear them. They also keep detailed records of their encounters. Many of them collect alimony or child support from male officers who foolishly knocked them up. Some of those badge bunnies also collect and spread sexually transmitted diseases. Women, whether they want to be your wife, your girlfriend, or just a one night stand, pose a substantial risk to your mental, physical, and financial health, as well as a risk to your reputation.

Another hazard of working with female officers is the generally predatory nature of females. As many careless male officers have discovered, women become cops for reasons that rarely have anything to do with a desire to fight crime or protect their community. Some of them are radical feminists who want to prove that they can do anything a man can do. Some of them want to be in a position to exercise authority over men. Some of them are looking for opportunities to sue their employer on bogus charges of sexual harassment or hostile workplace. If they do, they can get you fired and reward themselves with a healthy financial settlement. Some women view police agencies as hunting grounds for a male provider. They'll lure foolish male officers into sexual relationships to get knocked up, get married, quit their jobs, and then file for divorce a few years later so they can get alimony and half of his pension. Even if they can't get the man to marry, they'll still have him locked into eighteen years of child support.

Law enforcement is a magnet for lesbians. I would estimate that more than half of the female officers I worked with were lesbian or bisexual. They certainly represented a disproportionately higher percentage when compared to the general population. Whether they were dealing with coworkers or criminals, I found them to be unnecessarily belligerent and argumentative. Other male officers I have known made the same observations.

If you're a married man who is a cop or is hoping to become a cop, you should know that you have a better chance of being struck by lightning than having your marriage survive your career. Here are a few other reasons not to marry.

Women are chameleons and perpetual children. Even if you marry one who on the surface seems to be a psychologically stable adult, sooner or later her inner Godzilla will rear its ugly head. She will begin badgering you about how your job is affecting her. "You don't spend enough time with me!" or "You always work on holidays!" or "You never want to go out with our friends and family!" There is likely some validity to her complaints. There isn't much you can do about working on holidays. Aside from firefighters and emergency medical service workers, law enforcement officers are about the only government employees who provide face-to-face hands-on services 24 hours a day, 365 days of the year. Working on holidays is part of the job. Her complaining that you don't spend enough time with her will make you want to spend even less time with her. And, being completely self-absorbed, it will never occur to her that you are so physically and emotionally exhausted from the stresses of dealing with idiots on duty that you won't want to socialize or deal with idiots when you're off-duty. And, after you spend a few years on the job, you'll begin to realize that most of the people she expects you to socialize with are idiots. That includes immediate family members and other blood relatives. Being a cop forces you to see, hear, smell, touch, and taste the realities of the fallen human condition that people outside of the profession rarely experience and go out of their way to avoid. Having to listen to these sanctimonious ignoramuses express their opinions about the causes of and cures for societies problems is as annoying as a poke in the eye with a sharp stick. And when you finally have your fill of hearing them, and you tell them that they are idiots who don't know what they're talking about, having them personally insult you by telling you how jaded and negative you are and how you need to seek professional mental health counseling is intolerable. You'll finally realize that, as one internet blogger put it, "When family gatherings start to become an uncomfortable hassle, it's time to stop going." You can be sure that when these issues become so important to your wife that she insists on discussing them with you, she will wait until you're about to walk out the door to go on duty. So, instead of having a calm, clear, and focused mind when you go on duty, your blood pressure will be hovering near stroke territory and you will be too angry and distracted to focus on your job because she intentionally aggravated you as you were walking out the door. Working night shift and trying to sleep during the day is difficult enough when you're alone in a dark and quiet room. Trying to sleep while being relentlessly hounded by an implacable harpy and screaming children is simply impossible. I knew a few guys who were able to survive that situation and finally retire. To the best of my knowledge, most of them died from heart attacks or strokes within a few years of retiring. Whatever benefit a woman brings into your life will be completely overshadowed by the chronic drama and demands that she unnecessarily brings with it.

KNOW YOUR LIMITATIONS

In "Magnum Force," the third in the Dirty Harry movie series, Harry's boss and nemesis, Lt. Briggs, patronizingly boasts, "I never had to take my gun out of its holster once. I'm proud of that."

Harry replies, "You're a good man lieutenant. A good man always knows his limitations." In the context of the movie, Harry's reply was a subtle insult. In the real world, Harry's reply is sound wisdom. Taking a calculated risk to protect the life of a brother officer or the life of an innocent person when you know that the odds are not in your favor is courageous. Carelessly and unnecessarily rushing headlong into the arms of the grim reaper just to prove your bravado is stupidity. Some officers have difficulty distinguishing between the two. Physical and psychological injuries nearly always result when people exceed their physical and psychological limitations. As an officer, just because you have a star or a shield on your uniform shirt does not mean that you have a big red "S" underneath it. You need to be aware of your limitations and learn how to compensate for them. Spend some time honestly assessing those limitations. Learn how to think outside the box. There is often more than one way to solve a problem or accomplish a task. Keep an open mind and don't let brute force become your default solution. Stop watching violent fictional cop movies and television programs. They will warp your perception of reality and cause you to inaccurately assess your options and your limitations. If you end up crippled or disabled because you overestimated and exceeded your limitations, you will be of no use to yourself or other people who need your help. Do not use the abilities and limitations of your coworkers to measure your own. Figure out what your own natural strengths and weaknesses are. Develop your strengths and learn how to compensate for your weaknesses. That will make you a better officer and a happier human being. It will also increase the likelihood that you will be able to collect your pension and enjoy it.

AVOID PORNOGRAPHY

"Sow a thought and you reap an action; sow an act and you reap a habit; sow a habit and you reap a character; sow a character and you reap a destiny."
- Ralph Waldo Emerson, 1803 – 1882,
American essayist, lecturer, philosopher, and poet.

The culture in which you live will constantly be putting subtle and not so subtle pornographic images and ideas in front of you. The nature of the job also increases the possibility that you will be involuntarily exposed to pornography during investigations, search warrants, and arrests. Porn is addictive, and even the most seemingly innocuous movies, television programs, and advertisements have some subtle pornographic or sexually provocative element to try to enslave you so you will keep coming back for more. As officers, you spend much of your day in a virtual sewer. Why would you want to use your off-duty time remaining in that sewer? Find some healthy hobbies to occupy your eyes and your mind. There are hundreds of other things that are more useful and satisfying than looking at whatever the entertainment industry's puppet masters of porn are peddling. A few hours with the guys restoring an old car, practicing defensive tactics, whittling, woodworking, playing in a band, shooting hoops, camping, fishing, playing poker, scuba diving, meditating, etc. are all infinitely safer and more satisfying than getting wrecked in some topless bar, or watching the lurid stupidity that pours from television and movies like water from a broken fire hydrant.

DON'T TAKE THE BAIT

People are going to bait you to try make you lose control of your emotions. They could be criminals, or news reporters, or social justice warriors. Or they could be people hired by someone that you arrested (or hired by the attorney of that person) to try to get you to discredit yourself and get fired before trial. Do I think an attorney would do something like that? Not all of them. But enough of them to make it a legitimate concern if the charges against their client are serious enough and the stakes are high enough. For attorneys, good and evil or right and wrong are subjective philosophical abstraction. Winning their case is all that matters to most of them. So whenever someone baits you, don't assume they are just being an idiot. Assume that they have a darker purpose in mind. Don't respond to people who bait you. Just walk away.

AVOID SOCIAL MEDIA

Avoid posting comments or photos on social media sights. Facebook, Twitter, Instagram, TikTok and similar sites are mine fields. Comments you post today could come back to bite you years from now. The internet is fine if you are using it for investigative research, educational purposes, catching up on news, email, shopping, paying bills, or similar time saving conveniences. But trolling or responding to trolls on social media sites is very risky. And, as I mentioned early in this work, if someone is offended by something that you post, they might complain to your boss. Even if you don't get fired, the resulting investigation will be more aggravating than it is worth.

TAKE CARE OF YOUR HEALTH

"To keep the body in good health is a duty...otherwise we shall not be able to keep the mind strong and clear."

- Buddha

"It is health that is the real wealth, and not pieces of gold and silver."

- Mahatma Gandhi

If you were not naturally endowed with great physical and intellectual abilities, that does not mean that you cannot be a good officer by making the most of what you were born with. If you develop disciplined exercise, dietary, and study habits, you can become a valuable asset to your agency. But be honest with yourself. Being a cop isn't for everyone. If, after you get the job, you realize that you made a mistake and that you aren't cut out for it, there is no shame in quitting. You'll earn more respect from your coworkers and your boss by admitting it than you will by staying in and making an embarrassing or deadly mistake.

STEROIDS

Do not get sucked into taking anabolic steroids. I've known numerous officers who have taken steroids to bulk up and increase their size and strength for professional reasons. Steroids must be prescribed by a doctor. If you have to be drug tested and you test positive for steroids that were not prescribed and administered by a doctor, you might find yourself unemployed. Ever hear of "Roid Rage?" It's a real thing. Steroid users deny it exists. But numerous studies clearly show that steroids increase irritability and aggression. I've personally witnessed those personality changes in officers who were on steroids. Irritability and aggression are not good personality traits for people who must keep a cool head under stressful conditions. Here are some other possible side effects of anabolic steroid use: High blood pressure, blood clots, heart attacks, stroke, artery damage, decreased sperm production, enlarged breasts, shrinking testicles, male-pattern baldness, testicular cancer, compromised immune system, mania, delusions, severe acne, cysts, and jaundice. If you're a steroid aficionado, don't tell me that those studies are nonsense. Sure, the steroids work. Some officers who take them can have a couple of good years. But after those few years go by, those officers often suffer more rapid physical and psychological decline than their non-steroid using coworkers. More than a few of them have to retire early because of related physical or mental health problems.

YOU ARE WHAT YOU EAT

If you eat fast foods from drive-thru windows or sit-down meals in restaurants where you cannot see your food for the entire time it is being prepared and transported to your table, it is only a matter of time before you unwittingly ingest drugs, poison, saliva, snot, semen, urine, fecal matter, or blood from some cook or server who intentionally included one or more of those unwanted condiments in your order because they hate cops.

When I was assigned to a criminal investigations unit, a probation officer stopped by our office one morning to give us his monthly update of who was under his supervision in our area. I asked him if there was a restaurant in our community that did not have at least one of his clients working there. He took a minute to review his paper work and then replied, "If you had asked me that yesterday I could have said yes. But, as of this morning, the answer is no."

There are some nice honest people in the food service industry. But people who are on parole or probation tend to have limited employment options, and restaurants tend to have high employee turnover rates. So food service industry employment is an attractive option for people who are on parole or probation. Those people are sometimes high school dropouts, low achievers, or people with serious personality disorders. One or more of those attributes is what got them arrested and placed on probation in the first place. As much as they would like to walk up to you and spit in your face, they know that doing so would get them sent back to jail. Standing a few feet away and watching you bite into a burger that has his or her "special sauce" on it is the next best thing.

Bringing your meals from home is the best practice. If that isn't possible, there are grocery stores and supermarkets that have foods prepared in advance, packaged, sealed, and placed in display cases where you can safely retrieve them. Some of them have sandwich shops where you can watch as your food is being prepared.

CHOOSE YOUR FRIENDS WISELY

"Associate yourself with men of good quality if you esteem your own reputation; for 'tis better to be alone than in bad company."

- George Washington, 1732 – 1799

"Do not be deceived. Bad company corrupts good morals."

- 1 Corinthians 15:33, NASB

Propositions like these occur so often, in so many different languages, and in such a wide variety of religious and philosophical contexts throughout history, you would be foolish to ignore them. The people you associate with will have an influence on what you believe and how you behave. And, even if they don't have an influence, other people will form an opinion of you by the company you keep. Who are men of good character? Men who encourage you when you do well; who try to help you improve when do not; and whose personal and professional lives are consistent with the high values they profess. Anyone who tries to lure you into doing something that your conscience or common sense tells you is wrong or is unnecessarily risky is bad company. That can include other officers, supervisors, or administrators. When you figure out who those people are, avoid socializing with them, and work with them only as necessary. And, if you see one of them commit a criminal act for which he could be criminally charged, or a breach of policy that could get him fired, you have a choice; report the event to the appropriate person in your chain of command, or be implicated as an accessory after the fact when their transgression and your knowledge of it come to light. I'm not guessing about this. I've seen otherwise good officers lose their careers for withholding information or lying about the transgressions of other officers. If the thought of turning in a bad cop bothers you, just remember that the people who dislike you for being an informer aren't going to pay your mortgage, your car payments, or your health insurance when you are unemployed. If your coworkers understand that you will not risk your job, your reputation, or your families well-being by covering for their intentional acts of malfeasance or misfeasance, they will probably avoid putting you in that position. Tell them not to do things in your presence that could get them in trouble, and tell them not to tell you about it afterwards if they do. Honest plausible deniability is a valuable asset. The less time you spend around people who do stupid things, the better your chances of having that deniability and keeping your job.

KEEP A DIARY

People and events you encounter during your tour of duty should be documented in a diary. That includes anything or anyone. Cases you work on; interaction with people in your community; or interactions or disputes that you could have with other officers or supervisors. Keep your diary off duty. An argument might be made that a diary maintained on duty is work product and subject to public record laws. If the diary is made off duty for your personal use, it is not work product and not subject to public record disclosure. I found that an electronic diary in the form of e-mails to myself was especially useful. Why? The date and time stamps on emails are put there by the service provider. You can't alter them. So you cannot credibly be accused of backdating or doctoring the entries for selfish purposes. There is a permanent electronic record unless you delete it. Here's how it works. Throughout your tour of duty, make notes in a text document on your cellphone. Record anything that you think could be interesting or important. When your shift ends and you are officially off duty, copy and paste the text into an email to yourself. Make sure you include some off duty notes not related to work. Things like brief notes about shopping, doctor visits, or recreational activity. Hit send. There it is; solid evidence of your diary entry. When it arrives in your email, delete the entry from your cellphone and empty the trash. If the time stamp on the diary entry clearly shows that it was made when you were off duty, and it includes notes about off duty personal activity, and you claim the diary is personal, I believe there is a good chance that any attempt to force you to disclose its contents would be rejected by a judge. Store your diary entries in a separate "Diary" file in your email account. If you're concerned about your account provider crashing and losing the emails, consider sending a carbon copy to a secondary / backup account with another provider. If you don't have a backup account, print hard copies of the email each time you send one. Put the hard copies in a file.

CASE LAW

Stay up to date on case law and changes in statutes, county ordinances and municipal ordinances. Saying, "Duh. . . I don't know," when asked about something that you should know doesn't instill much confidence from citizens or supervisors. And it doesn't instill much confidence from jurors when you're being grilled on the witness stand by a sharp aggressive defense attorney. Most agencies post bulletins about case law and statute changes. It probably won't take more than five or ten minutes a day to read those bulletins.

TRAIN REGULARLY

In addition to my adjunct instructor position at a regional criminal justice institute, I was one of the firearms training officers at one of my departments. Since the department supplied the targets and ammo, the other training officer and I encouraged officers to train regularly. Once every couple of months we would schedule an "open range" day so officers could come to practice and get some additional help if they needed it. All it would cost them was their time. The lack of interest most officers had in showing up at the range for an hour to do a little practice was disappointing, especially in light of how often they complained about a lack of training opportunities. In spite of us notifying officers well in advance, there were several open range days where no one showed up. On days when they did show up, their performance was less than good. Shooting is a perishable skill that requires practice. If your agency provides you with ammo, targets, and a range, take advantage of it. If they don't, it's still your life on the line and your responsibility to train.

If your department has a SWAT Team, they probably train together regularly. But how long will it take your SWAT Team to respond if a bad situation erupts that your squad is forced to deal with immediately? How many events have you heard of in the past twenty years in which two or three patrol officers had to respond to situations that required immediate intervention and a swat team was not available. I've seen numerous videos of three or four officers suddenly finding themselves in circumstances where some armed individual made a furtive move that prompted all of the officers to open fire. Were the shootings legally justified? Yes. Could those situations have been handled better? With regular training and a bit of advance planning, I believe they could. If four of you show up at a scene where someone is armed, why not have two officers as predetermined designated shooters who tactically position themselves accordingly? Having an armed individual disabled or killed by four or five well placed shots by two of the four well trained squad members looks better than an individual being riddle to death in hail of gunfire by four officers, regardless of how well justified the shooting is. It greatly reduces the possibility of collateral damage by all of the rounds that miss in a spray and pray scenario where everyone is firing as much in response to hearing everyone else firing as from the legitimate threat posed by the individual. It saves the crime scene unit from having to deal with the nightmare of trying to find all of the rounds that missed the target in a spray and pray scenario. And, since every officer who fires is going to be placed on administrative leave until the investigation can determine where everyone's bullets went, whose bullets were responsible for collateral damage, and whose bullets took down the threat, two officers taking care of business avoids having to pay out massive amounts of overtime to officers who are working beyond safe fatigue limits due to staff shortages caused by an entire squad being on administrative leave. If you agree, suggest the idea to your agency's chief or training unit supervisor. If they are opposed to the idea, talk to your squad members about it and come up with a plan that you can all agree upon.

Defensive tactics is another area where officer interest in training is disappointing. I can understand if you don't want to spend your off-duty time with your coworkers. You have your own life to live off duty. But considering what is at stake when you are on duty, it would be to the advantage of you and your squad members to spend an hour or two each week doing defensive tactics training and scenarios together, even if it means coming in an hour early once a week. Not only will it help each of you sharpen your own skills, it will help you learn each other's strengths and weaknesses. Knowing that can help you compensate for each other when two or more of you actually do have to get involved together in physical confrontations with uncooperative suspects. Like shooting, your defensive tactics skills will degrade if you don't practice them. Waiting until you get into a hand to hand struggle with someone is not a good time to try to remember appropriate techniques or rely on instinct and muscle memory. You'd be surprised what an hour of serious training with each other once a week can do for you as a team.

MIND YOUR OWN BUSINESS

Cops are problem solvers by nature. That's good. But many of the problems that cops are called upon to solve are not law enforcement or public safety issues. They are sometimes people's personal problems that are none of your business. Just because you get dispatched to a call does not mean that you have to take action or solve the problem when you arrive. Carefully evaluate the situation before getting in too deep. Sometimes it's best to refer people to other organizations or professionals such as psychologist, clergymen, or social service agencies that are better equipped to deal with the problem. For example: One afternoon I was on patrol through a mall parking lot when I was flagged down by a stylishly dressed woman frantically waiving her arms. She was standing beside a late model European luxury sedan. She was in a panic because she locked her keys in her car and was going to be late for a business appointment. She was aware that some officers carried car opening tools with their equipment. I happened to be one of those officers. The woman asked me if I could unlock her car. I assessed the situation and told her that I could, but that I would not. She furiously asked, "Why not?!" I explained that the county had numerous private citizens who had invested thousands of dollars in training, tools, office space, telephone directory advertisements, and occupational licenses to be locksmiths. I told her that I didn't think it was fair for a government employee who was paid by a locksmith's tax dollars to compete with the locksmith by providing locksmith services for free. I had a phone directory in my cruiser and I told her that she was welcome to use it to call one of those locksmiths. She angrily stormed back into the mall and telephoned the sheriff's office to complain about my refusing to help her. Fortunately, my supervisor was on my side. There were a few occasions under similar circumstances where I broke that rule. If there was a child or animal in distress inside the car and I could quickly open it without breaking a window was one such circumstance. Or if the person was trying to get to work, but was clearly too poor to afford a locksmith. In those cases the locksmith lost nothing because the person wouldn't have been able to pay them anyway. And helping someone get to their job by unlocking their car for them gained a ton of goodwill for the department.

There are other times when minding your own business is more important. For instance, when people call 911 because they are having a civil or domestic dispute with someone else, but no crime has been committed. If you try to mediate the dispute, the odds are high that one of the parties is going to be dissatisfied with the solution you offer. No matter how rational and reasonable the solution you offer is, your uniform lends the color of law to it. If you're going to try to mediate a dispute between people, you'd better tell them in advance that you are only making suggestions to try to help them, and that you have no authority to compel them to accept the solution that you offer. And, unless you have a ton of experience in dispute resolution, you're probably better off advising them to find an impartial mediator that they can both trust to help them solve the problem. If the dispute is heated and those involved are being loud and verbally aggressive with each other, so what? Don't interfere. People have a constitutional right to have loud verbal disagreements as long as they are not causing a breach of peace that meets the criteria of a criminal statute. Rather than try to mediate angry but legal disputes, a technique that I often used that seemed to work was to step back and saying nothing. I let them yell at each other until one or both of them noticed that I wasn't saying anything. When they asked what I was going to do, I told them that I was going to stand there and wait until one of them got angry or stupid enough to take a poke at the other. I told them that I would then arrest the aggressor, take them to jail, and wouldn't have to come back later for round two of their battle. That usually embarrassed them enough to settle their dispute more quietly.

KNOW YOUR AGENCY'S POLICIES

Law enforcement agencies have policy and procedure manuals. Several agencies that I worked for had manuals that were six or seven hundred pages long. That manual is one of the first pieces of equipment that agencies issue to new officers. Usually included with the manual is a form that the officers have to sign when they receive the manual. That form says something to the effect that the officer has read the manual and agrees to abide by its contents. Reading and digesting the contents of a seven-hundred page policy and procedure manual in five or ten minutes was beyond my skill set.

Reading and remembering everything in a policy and procedure manual can be such a daunting task that some officers toss it into the their locker or the trunk of their cruiser and forget about it. Don't do that. Even if you can only wade through a few pages a day, force yourself to read it. If you look at the table of contents, you will probably notice that some policies and procedures are more important than others. Start by learning the important ones. Policies and procedures that deal with arrests, use of force, use of weapons, reports, etc. are things that can get you into big trouble if you don't know them. When you have those pretty well memorized, learn the more trivial policies and procedure that might get you in a little trouble, but won't get you fired if you break one of them.

If you know how to use it, the policy and procedure manual can be your friend. How so? Because the people who are most likely to try to cause you trouble don't know your policies and procedures. You'll usually be safe from their attempts as long as you can show that you were acting within the scope of your policies and procedures. If the policies and procedures don't specifically tell you that you must do something, you probably have a defense for not doing it. If they tell you that you are supposed to do something that someone doesn't like, you're probably safe if you do it. Policies and procedures help an agency run smoothly. But that isn't their only purpose. They are also designed to protect the agency from liability if you breach a policy and someone or something is harmed as a result.

CODE OF ETHICS

The number of officers killed in the line of duty each year doesn't even come close to the number of officers who get fired for committing acts that are clear violations of their code of ethics. For the last twenty years of my career I kept a copy of that code hanging on the wall of the man-cave where I dressed for work. I took that code seriously. That didn't stop a few bad things from happening to me. But those bad things were caused by unethical coworkers and bosses who did not take the code seriously. Some of them completely ignored it. On more than one occasion I had coworkers or bosses whose personal dislike for me motivated them to try to harm me professionally and personally. Whatever damage they were able to do was only temporary. In spite of their efforts, things providentially worked out to my advantage in the long run. I landed on my feet in a better place. I was finally able to retire with an adequate pension in spite of the personal malice of those coworkers and bosses. Here is the code that was in effect when I began my career:

> "As a law enforcement officer, my fundamental duty is to serve mankind; to safeguard lives and property; to protect the innocent against deception, the weak against oppression or intimidation and the peaceful against violence or disorder; and to respect the constitutional rights of all men to liberty, equality, and justice.
>
> I will keep my private life unsullied as an example to all;

maintain courageous calm in the face of danger, scorn or ridicule; develop self-restraint; and be constantly mindful of the welfare of others.

Honest in thought and deed both in my personal and official life, I will be exemplary in obeying the law and the regulations of my department. Whatever I see or hear of a confidential nature or that is confided to me in my official capacity will be kept ever secret unless revelation is necessary in the performance of my duty.

I will never act officiously or permit personal feelings, prejudices, animosities or friendships to influence my decisions. With no compromise for crime and with relentless prosecution of criminals, I will enforce the law courteously and appropriately without fear or favor, malice or ill will, never employing unnecessary force or violence and never accepting gratuities.

I recognize the badge of my office as a symbol of public faith, and I accept it as a public trust to be held so long as I am true to the ethics of police service.

I will constantly strive to achieve these objectives and ideals, dedicating myself before God to my chosen profession… law enforcement."

The current code has a few minor word additions to original version. Personally, I don't think the changes added anything of value.

CONCLUSION

No doubt this work will disturb a few people. No matter. Those people were probably already disturbed before they read it. But if I've been able to make a few critics re-evaluate their beliefs and reduce their hostilities, or make a few citizens more aware of the difficulties we face, or encourage a few officers to adjust their priorities so they can live long enough to retire with their physical and mental health intact, it was worth the effort.

www.ingramcontent.com/pod-product-compliance
Lightning Source LLC
Chambersburg PA
CBHW050910260726
48660CB00001B/130